MARCO  POLO

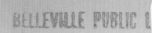

W9-CDN-209

CAN ADA EAST

MONTRÉAL TORONTO QUÉBEC

FREE!

THE TOURING APP

shows you the way...
including routes and offline maps!

GET MORE OUT OF YOUR MARCO POLO GUIDE

IT'S AS SIMPLE AS THIS

1 go.marco-polo.com/cae

2 download and discover

GO!

WORKS OFFLINE!

SYMBOLS

INSIDER TIP Insider Tip

★ Highlight

●●●● Best of ...

☆ Scenic view

☺ Responsible travel: fair
trade principles and the
environment respected

(*) Telephone numbers
that are not toll-free

**PRICE CATEGORIES
HOTELS**

Expensive over C$240
Moderate C$130–240
Budget under C$130

Rates are per double room
without breakfast. Children
usually sleep in their parents'
room for free

**PRICE CATEGORIES
RESTAURANTS**

Expensive over C$35
Moderate C$25–35
Budget under C$25

The prices are for a main
meal in the evening, including taxes. At lunchtime it is
much cheaper

CONTENTS

DID YOU KNOW?
Timeline → p. 14
For bookworms and film buffs
→ p. 24
Local specialities → p. 28
Mennonites: an old-fashioned
life → p. 42
Poutine – hot & greasy → p. 80
Alexander Graham Bell → p. 88
Budgeting → p. 134
Weather → p. 136

MAPS IN THE GUIDEBOOK
(148 A1) Page number and
coordinate in road atlas
(0) Location/address is outside of the map section
(U A1) Coordinates for the
map of Montréal in the inside
back cover
Map of Toronto → p. 37
Map of Ottawa → p. 52
Map of Québec → p. 77

(𝄞 A–B 2–3) Refers to the
removable pull-out map
(𝄞 a–b 2–3) Refers to the
additional map on the pull-
out map

INSIDE FRONT COVER:
The best Highlights

INSIDE BACK COVER:
Map of Montréal

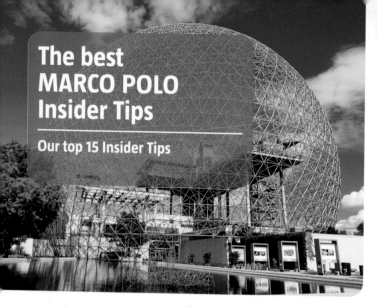

The best MARCO POLO Insider Tips

Our top 15 Insider Tips

INSIDER TIP Enjoy art on Lake Ontario

Traditional glass-blowers and sculptors, dance performances, concerts and numerous festivals in the *York Quay Centre* in Toronto's harbour → p. 36

INSIDER TIP The ultimate test of courage in Toronto

Adrenaline high: without a railing and with just a thin steel cable you can take the *EdgeWalk* on the *CN Tower* high above the city → p. 35

INSIDER TIP Hungry for beavertail?

At the *Byward Market* in Ottawa you can try beavertails, which is a type of fried pastry that is sprinkled with sugar and cinnamon → p. 53

INSIDER TIP Surfing

A different kind of surfing: in the *Tidal Bore Rafting Park* you will ride a tidal bore in a rubber dinghy → p. 112

INSIDER TIP Canoe through a canyon

The canyon of the *Parc national des Hautes-Gorges* in Québec is every bit as impressive as the Rockies → p. 71

INSIDER TIP Clowns and performers in Montréal

The circus school *La Tohu* trains jugglers, mimes and tightrope artists and up-and-coming talent from all over the world – and also gives performances → p. 63

INSIDER TIP Native American cuisine

Sagamité restaurant on the outskirts of Québec City serves refined Native American/Huron cuisine with lots of wild berries and other regional ingredients → p. 79

INSIDER TIP Visit the belugas

Tadoussac on the northern shore of St Lawrence is regarded as one of the best places for whale watching in the world. This is the southernmost habitat of the white whales → p. 82

INSIDER TIP **Hike with panoramic views**

The *Coastal Trail* in the Fundy National Park winds along the rugged coast where the tide fluctuates over 10 m/32.8 ft → **p. 90**

INSIDER TIP **Log cabins by the ocean**

The long journey is worth it: with a little luck whales will cavort about in the sea in front of your cabin in the *Phare de Pointe-des-Monts* in Québec → **p. 122**

INSIDER TIP **Icebergs in the summer**

On the northern coast of Newfoundland near *Twillingate,* massive icebergs drift past from early summer to mid-July → **p. 103**

INSIDER TIP **The longest hiking trail in the world**

The Trans Canada Trail will stretch over 18,000 km/11,200 mi − the starting section, the already completed *East Coast Trail* in Newfoundland is especially beautiful → **p. 102**

INSIDER TIP **An insight into the eco-system**

The interactive exhibitions in the *Biosphère* in Montréal − on the former World Fair Expo 67 grounds − show the fascinating background of the Great Lakes, alternative energy, major environmental issues such as climate change and sustainable technologies (photo left) → **p. 61**

INSIDER TIP **Big screen for sport fans**

Sporty Toronto: whether it is ice hockey, football or baseball, in the large *Real Sports* bar next to the Rogers Centre, all the big league games are broadcast and celebrated → **p. 41**

INSIDER TIP **Québec's best delicacies**

Cheese and caviar, liqueurs and pies − the gourmet market *Le Marché des Saveurs* in Montréal stocks only the best products from all over the province − and the vibrant city market is just across the street → **p. 65**

BEST OF ...

FOR FREE

● *Toronto's avantgarde for free*
Young art can be visited free of charge in Toronto: the *Power Plant Gallery* in the York Quay Centre on Toronto's waterfront curates four large-scale exhibitions every year displaying design, photography and architecture by young artists → p. 36

● *Marvel at waterfalls*
Canada's natural wonders and magnificent landscapes can be seen in the national parks, which have entrance fees. But not at the most famous: *Niagara Falls.* However, there is a fee for the parking → p. 48

● *Free music in Ottawa*
The nation's capital splashes out almost every weekend during the summer when it celebrates different festivals – be it blues, jazz or Canada Day. These free concerts are funded by the *National Capital Commission* → p. 48

● *Dancing dolls in Montreal*
This is not great art and the dolls don't actually dance, but the *Barbie Expo (photo)* in Montreal is still well worth a visit: hundreds of Barbie dolls are displayed dressed in haute couture and the exhibition is free of charge. → p. 60

● *Halifax: Sundays in the park*
In Halifax, Sunday afternoons are typically spent in the park. During the summer there are free concerts in the colourful greenery of the *Public Gardens*, only a few steps from the citadel → p. 93

● *Sunrise over the Atlantic*
The people on Newfoundland could set up a box office on the winding road to *Signal Hill.* Luckily for you, they don't. In the port of St John you can admire the finest and earliest sunrise in the New World, every morning, always free of charge → p. 101

ONLY IN EASTERN CANADA
Unique experiences

● *Paddling on Lake Opeongo*

Lakes, moose, cliffs, woods and solitude – that is the Canada that we all imagine. And on a canoe trip in the *Algonquin Provincial Park* you can live the dream – a tent and sleeping bag are available to rent (photo) → p. 45

● *Dinner with a view*

The *Cape d'Or Lighthouse* is perched on a high cliff above the Bay of Fundy and provides stunning panoramic views. This is where you can watch one of the largest tidal fluctuations in the world. The small restaurant next to the lighthouse serves typically Canadian fare – such as hearty chowder – and the freshest fish → p. 90

● *Through Montréal by bike*

Experience Montréal like a local – by bicycle. From the old town along the St Lawrence canals into the university district of St-Denis. Rent one of the affordable *Bixi Bikes* that you will find at many sites throughout the city → p. 64

● *Enjoy the scenery of the Atlantic*

Cape Breton Island offers the wildest, most unspoilt and most beautiful panoramas on the east coast. Along the almost 300 km/186 mi long circular road, the *Cabot Trail,* colourful fishing villages, rugged cliffs, lush valleys and scenic highlands are lined up one after another – ideal to experience on a guided bike tour → p. 86, 122

● *Canadian maritime pub*

The cosy harbour pub *Split Crow* in the old town of Halifax serves good beer and good music. A different band performs almost every night while the guests enjoy their fish and burgers. A great atmosphere → p. 92

● *Along the river of the whales*

The St Lawrence estuary is home to more whale species than anywhere else on our planet. Around the *Mingan Archipelago* you can see blue, fin and humpback whales and partake in scientific observations → p. 75

ONLY IN

BEST OF ...

● *Mourn the 'Titanic' in Halifax*
When the heavens open up a tour of artefacts from the 'Titanic' is very appropriate. Many reminders of the tragedy are preserved in the *Maritime Museum* (and in several cemeteries) → p. 91

● *Underground shopping*
Spend a rainy day in Montréal's *Ville Souterraine* without ever having to go outside. Almost 2000 shops and restaurants offer plenty of variety and lots of shopping fun (photo) → p. 65

● *Lighthouse ahoy!*
Bad weather also has its good side in *Peggy's Cove* and the other small harbour villages along the south coast of Nova Scotia. The typical fog that swirls around the craggy harbours ensures particularly atmospheric photos → p. 93

● *Ride the Niagara River rapids*
It does not matter what the weather is like when you are on an exciting, high-powered *Whirlpool Jetboat Tour* through the towering rapids – you are going to get wet anyway! → p. 126

● *Vikings in Newfoundland*
Fog and drizzle in *L'Anse aux Meadows,* on the northern tip of Newfoundland, are not uncommon. However, inside the replicated Viking cabins, you can get cosy on the fur benches next to the campfire, listening to the 'residents' tell the old sagas → p. 100

● *In the Royal Ontario Museum*
No matter how long it rains, time flies in Toronto's largest museum. Here, despite the name, you will not see any royalty. But you will see mummies, dinosaurs and a massive five-storey crystal → p. 38

RAIN

RELAX AND CHILL OUT
Take it easy and spoil yourself

● *Greenery meets music in Toronto*

A stroll along the water is always relaxing. In Toronto's harbour there is even a *Music Garden*. Its layout with perennials and grasses was inspired by a suite written by Johann Sebastian Bach. Unique! → p. 39

● *Therapeutic water and calming forests*

The *Scandinave Spa* in the Blue Mountains on Lake Huron is perfect for a day of pampering. Escape from your everyday world and enter into the serenity of a natural outdoor environment with hot and cold waterfalls, Finnish and eucalyptus sauna, numerous swimming pools and massage rooms. What more does a body need to relax? → p. 123

● *Islands in the Georgian Bay*

A hundred years ago it inspired painters – the rugged beauty of the *Georgian Bay Islands* in the Lake Huron. Sit back and enjoy the scenery on a half-day boat trip in the wake of chic yachts, which draw their bow waves between the islands → p. 48

● *Taste Niagara's wines*

The country's best wines come from the sunny climate of the Niagara Peninsula. You can taste the wines in about a dozen wineries around *Niagara-on-the-Lake* (photo) in a relaxed atmosphere – and stay over in the lovely Cape House B&B → p. 51

● *Massage on the waves*

The location of the *Bota Bota Spa* in Montréal is quite unusual: the treatments are offered on an old converted ferry in the harbour. You can enjoy five storeys with whirlpools, saunas and massage rooms → p. 63

● *Living in the 19th century*

You will never again feel as far away from modern civilisation as you will here: the old fishing village *Battle Harbour* is located on a tiny island off the Labrador coast. You sleep in old fishing houses, surrounded by nothing but beautiful nature, whales and icebergs → p. 101

CHILL OUT

INTRODUCTION

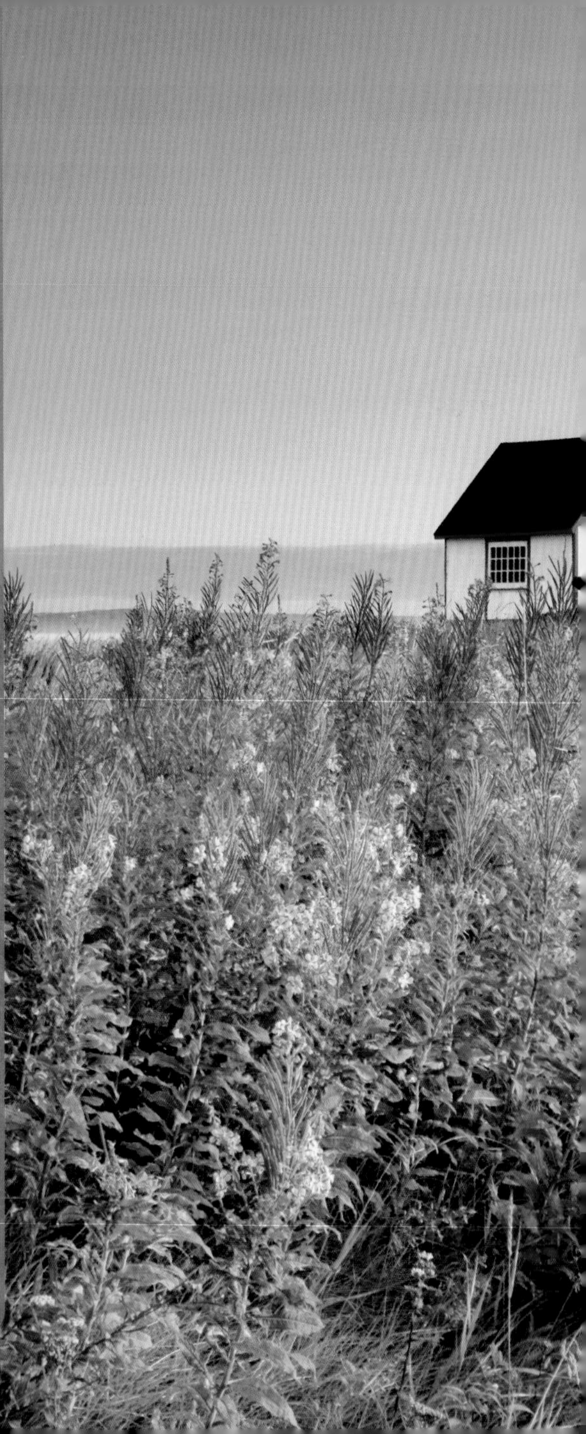

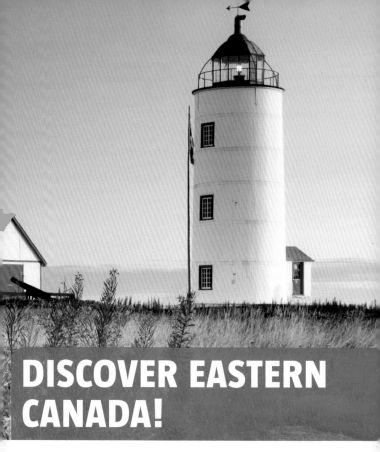

DISCOVER EASTERN CANADA!

During the past few years, Canada has become sexy: this has something to do with the young, dynamic Prime Minister Justin Trudeau and the cool metroplises, wild nature and great experiences offered by this country. What is more, Canadians are exemplary in many ways: they have created a magnificent system of national parks across the country, their schools are excellent and their businesses innovative and the country has participated in all UN peace missions throughout the world for many decades. Canadians are famed for their politeness and friendliness. These are all good reasons for planning a visit to the country!

The *Niagara Falls* and the richly coloured foliage of an *Indian Summer* are at the top of Eastern Canada's list of attractions. Deservedly so. Two absolute highlights. But there is a lot more to discover in this massive country: one of the world's highest towers in Toronto, hip and trendy shops in Montréal, and fine lobster restaurants on the Atlantic coast. Active holidaymakers will find their paradise in Canada's *outdoor country*: on canoe tours through the quiet landscape of the Algonquin Park, on a trip to the lighthouses of Nova Scotia, iceberg watching

Photo: Lighthouse on Île Verte, St Lawrence River

Always well attended: the restaurants on Rue St-Vincent in Old Montréal

in Newfoundland or on a beach hike to one of the highest tidal fluctuations in the world.

The scale of this country is hard to grasp from a European perspective. Canada is *the second largest country in the world* with a surface of almost 4 million mi². From the Atlantic to the Pacific it measures over 5500 km/3418 mi and spans six time zones. The eastern half of the country is as big as Western Europe from the North Cape of Norway to Gibraltar. Six times the size of the United Kingdom, the province of Québec (595,400 mi²) is the second largest province of Canada, and the second smallest province Ontario (415,600 mi²) is still four times the size of the United Kingdom. Yet only approximately 37 million people live in

About 35,000 BC
Paleo-Indian hunters migrate across the Bering Strait to North America

Around AD 1000
Vikings discover today's Labrador and Newfoundland

1497
John Cabot, the first European in modern times, sails to North America

1535/1536
Jacques Cartier discovers the St Lawrence River and uses the name Canada for the first time

1608
Samuel de Champlain establishes Québec

Canada – two thirds thereof in the eastern part. Statistically this means a population density of only four inhabitants per half a square mile – in Europe it is almost a hundred times more. In addition, most Canadians live in a narrow strip of only about 300 km/186 mi along the southern border of the United States. In the north you can drive for hours between towns – if there are roads, that is.

The English and the French were the most important settlers, however Germans, Italians and Ukrainians also settled here – and during the last few decades immigrants from Asia and the Caribbean have been on the increase. Canada favours a policy of *cultural tolerance*, meaning that is a 'melting pot of nations' like the United States, but a multicultural society.

It may be because Canada is still such a *young state* that the citizens are so proud of their history. Every town has wonderfully restored historic houses and at least one pioneer museum lovingly decorated with heirlooms. Especially attractive are the perfectly designed museum villages, which preserve the adventurous era of the pioneers. Here you will find living history where young Canadians enact the lives of their ancestors with real enthusiasm. In Nova Scotia you can marvel at France's first outposts in the New World in Port Royal and in the garrison town of Louisbourg. The fortresses of the colonial era have been preserved along the St Lawrence

> **Museum villages depict the adventurous era of the pioneers**

1670	1759	1867	1885	1901
Merchants from London establish the Hudson's Bay Company	The battle for Québec New France becomes an English crown colony	The birth of Canada: with the British North America Act, the colonies of Ontario, Québec, Nova Scotia and New Brunswick become the Dominion of Canada	Completion of the Trans-Canadian Railway	First radio link from Newfoundland to Europe

River in Québec City and Kingston. In the forests of the north, fur trading posts and mission stations – such as Old Fort William in Thunder Bay or Sainte-Marie among the Hurons near Midland – made the hard life in the wilderness bearable. Everything is larger, wider and wilder in Canada. While the Rocky Mountains in the west of Canada are well-known from postcards and picture books, the east impresses with its *dramatic coastal landscape* and the *Great Lake districts*. Out there on the Atlantic coast, the steep cliffs of Labrador and Newfoundland tower up from the sea. The people live in tiny fishing villages along the often storm-tossed coast, where icebergs pass in spring. The climate in the Atlantic provinces of Nova Scotia, Prince Edward Island and New Brunswick is far milder. Sparkling clean harbour towns lie along the rocky coast. Many of the inhabitants still survive off fishing and will serve you their delectable lobster. The densely forested mountain ranges in the hinterland form part of the *ancient Appalachian Mountains*, which glaciers from ice ages have eroded down to a soft low mountain range. Prince Edward Island, surrounded by red potato fields, boasts *the warmest and most beautiful seashore* in the country.

Toward the west the landscape joins the fertile St Lawrence lowlands, which used to be the great gateway to Canada, the route of explorers and fur traders. There, in the provinces of Québec and Ontario, lie the most important metropolises and *the economic heart* of the industrial nation. Québec City, Montréal, Toronto – the large cities of Canada are strung like pearls along the St Lawrence and Lake Ontario. They shine with postmodern architecture and a colourful mixture of ethnicities. And let us not forget the elegant capital Ottawa, with its numerous museums and manicured parks. And of course the thundering Niagara Falls, Eastern Canada's world-famous attraction.

> **World famous: the thunderous Niagara Falls**

North of the cities and the lush green farms of the lowlands starts *the silent realm of the many granite peaks and forests* of the Canadian Shield. Shaped like a giant horseshoe, this region of ancient rock was created by glaciers, which depressed the surface to create Hudson Bay and a region of thousands of lakes, untamed rivers and deep forests extending to the edge of the Arctic. The northern part of Ontario and Quebéc is a popular destination for fishermen, canoeists and wilderness enthusiasts.

1931
Canada acquires sovereignty in the British Commonwealth

1962
Completion of the Trans-Canada Highway, the first road from the Atlantic to the Pacific

1980/1995
After the Québec crisis in the 1970s, Québecers speak out against the secession

1997
Construction of the 13 km/8.1 mi long Confederation Bridge to Prince Edward Island

2017
Canada celebrates its 150th anniversary with festivals and great pomp

Given the immense expanse of Eastern Canada, the climate is surprisingly moderate. Apart from the coastal regions, where it is humid and temperate, a *continental climate* prevails in the entire eastern region. That means hot summers and bitterly cold, snowy winters. High in the north the summer is barely three months long, while in the south of Ontario on the Niagara Peninsula (almost on the same latitude as Florence) vineyards and peaches flourish.

Hot summers, bitter winters

If you come to Canada as a tourist, you will have an easy time: Eastern Canada offers an *excellent tourism infrastructure* with well-developed roads and clean hotels and motels. Museums and colourful markets, excellent restaurants, jazz clubs and trendy bistros make your stay in the cities entertaining. In the hinterland you will find secluded lodges and fishing camps to give you access to the wilderness.

'Iceberg ahead!' While kayaking in Newfoundland you often encounter bizarre ice formations

One can also experience many an adventure, be it on a canoe trip in the Algonquin Park, a hiking trip along the Cabot Trail in Nova Scotia or a kayak adventure on the rivers of Québec. However, you do not constantly have to push yourself to the limit: a musical in Toronto, a chin-wag in a bistro in Montréal, a shopping spree in one of the elegant malls – these are all part of a trip to Canada as well. A tour through the Laurentides or through the lake landscape of Ontario can also give you the feeling of freedom and vastness. Then, with the licking flames of a campfire during the red sunset, when a moose grazes in the reed grass at the edge of a shallow lake or a beaver paddles past, your stay becomes a dream holiday.

WHAT'S HOT

1 Chocolate meets beer

Quaffable Wine is not the only thing that grows in Canada, beer is also brewed – and the people are very proud of it. In *Benelux (245, Rue Sherbrooke Ouest | Montréal) (photo)* you get artisanal beer in a pitcher. Exotic creations like Chocolate Stout and Raspberry Blonde are offered at *Brutopia (1219, Rue Crescent | Montréal)*. At *L'amère à boire (2049, Rue St-Denis | Montréal)* you will find the appropriate food to go with the refined beer.

Ready for the stage

2

Up-and-coming Young authors and actors can count themselves lucky in Toronto. The 100-year-old *Alumnae Theatre Company (70 Berkeley St.) (photo)*, which is run by women, not only promotes up-and-coming female talent in the theatre world but also hosts the annual *New Ideas Festival*, where experimental pieces are performed. The *Factory Theatre (125 Bathurst St.)* even has an extra stage for experimental pieces. Further in the East, in Kingston, the *Domino Theatre (Harold Harvey Arena | 42 Church St.)* annually stages over a dozen pieces from the pens of young local writers.

3 Underground art

Creative Toronto and Montréal are the creative strongholds of the country – and this you will notice in passing. Like the artworks in the Montréal metro stations. For instance massive sculptures and colourful murals decorate the *Montmorency* station *(photo)*. Toronto's subway is also worth a visit: the artist Panya Clark Espinal created optical illusions in the *Bayview Station*. Even graffiti artists such as those from the *Graffiti Convention Under Pressure (www.underpressure.ca)* have left their (legal) mark.

There are lots of new things to discover in Eastern Canada. A few of the most interesting are listed below

'Holidays on Ice'

4

Winter nights Beyond the confines of hotel chains, artistically designed accommodation is setting new standards: Fogo Iceland is a beautiful spot in Newfoundland at the very edge of Canada. In the winter, the super luxurious *Fogo Island Inn (www.fogoislandinn.ca)* is really something special. It was built as part of an innovative art project on the coast that is fully enclosed by pack ice. This is where the Canadian winter is the wildest, and it can happen that a winter storm separates the island from the outside world for days. But Québec City has frosty nights too. During the dark months of the year, a completely frozen hotel opens its doors: the *Hotel de Glace (5930, Rue de la Faune | www.hoteldeglace-canada.com) (photo)* includes an ice bar, which is framed by sculptures, ice cream parlour and bedrooms with walls and beds made of ice.

Boozing in the underworld

5

Speakeasies A secret doorway, a password and a concealed room: the back rooms of bars enjoyed great popularity in America's prohibition era of the 1920s. The alcohol was frequently smuggled in from Canada. Almost a century later, speakeasies are making a comeback in Canada, for example the *Cloak Bar (488 Wellington St. | ww.thecloakbar.com)* with its British-styled elegance situated beneath the Marben Restaurant and offering special cocktails. The *Le 4E Mur (2021, Rue St. Denis | le4emur.com)* in Montreal retains its mystery – photography is forbidden in the club. The password is revealed in the sign-in on the website. The same also applies to the secret bar in the *Middle Spoon* restaurant in Halifax. Here a side door leads into *The Noble (1563 Barrington St. | themiddlespoon.ca/noble)*.

IN A NUTSHELL

BEAVERS AND MAPLES

Nature in all its glory: Eastern Canada offers an amazing natural spectacle at the end of September: the legendary Indian summer. Maples and other deciduous trees glow in all shades of red and orange after the first night frosts. A 1000 km/621 mi wide band of forest stretches across the whole of Canada: deciduous trees in the south and evergreens in the north, populated by numerous creatures including beavers, bears, lynx, deer, caribous and elks and even polar bears hunting seals in the swiftly decreasing pack ice in the far north of the Canadian Arctic.

ICE FREE FOR ZAMBONI

No other sport embodies the Canadian soul as well as ice hockey: during *Hockey Night*, the whole nation sits spellbound in front of the television. Children as young as five years learn to ice skate and what *Zamboni* is – a machine that resurfaces the ice in the ice rink. The professional players are heroes. Everybody knows them and the names of the legendary teams such as the *Canadiens de Montréal* or the *Toronto Maple Leafs*. However, Canada's official national sport is lacrosse, a fast ball game with Native American origins. Every major city has a team and in recent years the sport is once again back in vogue.

FIRST NATIONS

The descendents of the original inhabitants of Canada are no longer called Indians and Eskimos: the modern

This is how Canada ticks: the sacred independence of the Franco-Canadians – and other background issues

politically correct term is *First Nations*. Canadians now wish to acknowledge the presence of the 617 tribes that were in the country long before the settlers came. Their ancestors came across the Bering Strait into the north of America during the ice age. Over the course of millennia independent cultural groups emerged with semi-nomadic hunter tribes living in the north and far Eastern Canada. However, the Iroquois and Hurons had a sedentary woodland culture and settled in the region around the St Lawrence and

cultivated corn, beans and tobacco. Further to the west lived the bison hunting *Plains* tribes. Much later than the Native Americans, the ancestors of today's Inuit settled in Alaska from the Canadian Arctic about 1000 years ago. They call themselves the *Inuit* (people) and not *Eskimo*. The term 'Eskimo' translates as 'raw meat eater' and is considered derogatory.

The first decades of contact with the white settlers was not as traumatic for the Canadian natives as it was for their brothers in the United States. The fur traders were dependent on help from the Native Americans and had a limited impact on their way of life. However, diseases introduced by the Europeans decimated the tribes. Only with the settlement of the west during the 19th century were the Native Americans forced into reservations. After an improvement of their health care about 700,000 Native Americans and 50,000 Inuit live in Canada today.

NATIONAL PARKS

The most famous of Canada's 47 national parks, including Banff and Jasper, are situated in Western Canada. But there are some very beautiful natural areas in the east that are protected, such as the lakes of La Mauricie, the majestic Parc national de Forillon on the Gaspésie Peninsula, the mountains of Cape Breton Island or the fjords of Gros Morne in Newfoundland. *www. parkscanada.ca*

GOD SAVE THE QUEEN

A surprising and yet true fact: Queen Elizabeth II is Canada's head of state as the nation is a parliamentary democracy within the British Commonwealth. The Queen does however not have any power over the nation, but performs occasional ceremonial tasks and either she or the princes pay a visit to the country around every ten years. The Parliament in Ottawa is responsible for foreign policy, defence and finance. The ten Canadian provinces possess an extensive autonomy, for example in educational fields, cultural politics, healthcare and the exploitation of natural resources.

In a row: Inuits live in Labrador, Quebec in the Arctic and the north of Ontario

GROUP OF SEVEN

During colonial times the Canadian pioneers concerned themselves primarily with the business of survival. Therefore a creative cultural independence was only established during the 20th century. The first – and to this day most famous – Canadian painting style was established in 1912 when some young painters came together in Toronto and became known as the 'Group of Seven'. Inspired by the naturalist Tom Thomson, they developed a new, expressive form of landscape painting. Today their paintings fetch prices of up to 7 million dollars.

GOING GREEN

The then extemely industry-oriented government of Canada opted out of the Kyoto Protocoll in 2011. A sad indictment of one of the founding countries of Greenpeace and a move made primarily for financial reasons. However, many Canadians are very environmentally aware: waste is separated and recycled, nature parks are created and many environmental organisations are actively supported. Yet, compared to the rest of the world, the country remains one of the biggest offenders. Small wonder, since the Canadians have always had such a plentiful supply of resources. Mineral resources, energy and water are plentiful – and rethinking their ways takes time. It was not until 2015 that the new government under Justin Trudeau made a U-turn and undersigned the Paris Agreement.

JUSTIN, THE CHARMER

The new Prime Minister of Canada is young and sexy. He portrays himself as being in touch with the populace, lists boxing as his hobby and was a high school teacher prior to his election. Justin Trudeau is the new political star of Canada. His political talent is in his blood as the son of the former Prime Minister Pierre Trudeau who enjoyed great popularity during the 1970s and his hippy wife Margaret. Since his election in 2015, Justin has distinguished himself politically, brought women and minority individuals into the cabinet, retained a distance to Donald Trump and set up an airlift to bring Syrian refugees to Canada. He is also known for viral videos and photos as can be seen on YouTube.

NOUVELLE FRANCE

Bonjour! Anyone checking into a hotel or visiting a restaurant in Quebec is still greeted in French, despite the fact that the former colony passed to Great Britain over 250 years ago. The inhabitants of Quebec have retained their culture over the centuries and remain committed Francophiles. There is trouble if they are ignored even in small matters by Ottawa. The inhabitants of Quebec currently make up around 30 per cent of the population of Canada and it also helps a great deal if the Prime Minister originates from Montreal as is the case with Justin Trudeau.

Since then the linguistic and cultural division of Canada has repeatedly led to serious crises. Fifty years ago the nationalist *Parti Québécois* started to campaign for the secession of Québec from Canada; it even lead to terrorist attacks by separatists. Referendums were held in 1980 and 1995 and both times the majority of the population of Québec voted against independence – although it was very close.

'OUI' AND 'YES'

Canada is a bilingual nation. From the milk cartons in the supermarkets, the hiking map in the national parks to the entry forms at customs – everywhere the inscriptions are in both English and French. About 60 per cent of Canadians are English and about 30 per cent are French. However, the distribution is not even: in the Atlantic provinces, Ontario and in the west you will hear English almost exclusively, in Québec almost only French.

On a holiday trip to the predominantly French areas you will be fine, as many Canadians are bilingual. The English spoken here is more British in pronunciation and vocabulary than the American English spoken south of the border.

It gets more difficult in Québec, because *Québécois* goes back to old Norman and Breton dialects – and has a quite a few differences from modern French. It sounds rougher and more antiquated. Even the vocabulary varies: car *(*French *voiture)* in Québec is *le char,* shopping *(faire des courses)* is *magasiner,* and a tip *(pourboire)* in Québec is the very American *tip.*

F URRY CREATURES

You will not meet any grizzlies or polar bears on your trip through Eastern Canada. They are only found high in the Arctic and in the mountains of the west. There are, however, black bears: inquisitive and always hungry, they sniff through campsites at night, chase hikers from their blueberry territory or cross the Trans-Canada Highway. Always take your bear photos from a safe distance, store food in an airtight container in your car and immediately wash your dishes after eating that steak. Black bears have an excellent sense of smell and can hear very well, yet their sight is really bad.

R EDCOATS

The Mounties, the *Royal Canadian Mounted Police,* are probably Canada's most famous symbol – besides the maple leaf. Their red parade uniforms are seen at official events and appear in many souvenir photos. However, the 15,000 men of the *RCMP* are more than just colourful accessories: today, these highly trained police are responsible for

FOR BOOKWORMS & FILM BUFFS

Shadows on the Rock – Willa Cather's gripping portrayal of the hard times of the French colonists in New France. Nuns and prostitutes, settlers, trappers and convicts populate her novels, lovingly sketched out, but sometimes disconcerting (1931)

Take this Waltz – the Canadian indie director Sarah Polley paints a picture of a ménage-à-trois in Toronto, without kitsch and highly poetic. The title is taken from a song by Leonard Cohen (who died in 2016) which is interwoven into the film (2013)

The Shipping News – A fishing harbour in Newfoundland is the backdrop to this film (2001) by Lasse Hallström about the complicated life of Dan Quoyle. The novel by E. Annie Proulx is also well worth reading

Three Day Road – Joseph Boyden tells the story of a young Cree Indian who returns from the First World War and recovers with the stories of his aunt Niska (2006)

Snow Cake – A whimsical drama (2006) starring Sigourney Weaver and Alan Rickman and filmed in Wawa, Ontario

all the rural regions and places in Canada that cannot afford their own police.

TREASURES OF THE EARTH

Canada is immensely rich in natural resources: the ancient rock of the Canadian Shield, in northern Ontario, Québec and Labrador holds large deposits of iron, zinc, nickel and gold. The rivers of Québec provide virtually unlimited energy, and Newfoundland has oil. But Canada is trying to move away from its tradi-

export of natural resources seems like a sell-out of the country. Electricity from the huge hydroelectric power stations in Québec is sold to the United States at low prices while cheap wood from Ontario ends up as newspapers on breakfast tables all over the world.

SWEET DELIGHTS

It may be the cold winters that require high calorie foods or it may be that, since the days of the pioneers, people like to meet for a chat. But whatever

Be careful: don't take a bite! Canadians love their doughnuts so much that they are also used as a motif for picture frames

tional role as a supplier of raw materials for the world economy. Today, industrial production with its centre situated in southern Ontario around Toronto, Hamilton and Windsor makes up three quarters of the gross national product. Nevertheless, for many Canadians the

the reason, Canadians love their sweet donuts and their sweet coffee. The most popular place for both of these is the donut chain 'Tim Hortons', named after a famous ice hockey player. A sweet tip: try their French vanilla coffee and maple glazed donuts.

FOOD & DRINK

There is no Canadian national dish. The different immigrant groups that came from every continent were too different and the country too large.

Today the *diversity of specialities* is the charm of the multicultural food delight of Eastern Canada. In Toronto you can eat excellent Chinese, Ukrainian and Polish food. In Montréal you can have French, Portuguese, Jewish kosher food or sit in a bistro on the corner – just like in Paris. Of course the dishes that the country is famous for are also served: steaks from Alberta (with baked potatoes and corn on the cob with butter), lobster from the Atlantic coast and any number of variations of fresh salmon from the Pacific or Atlantic.

The *culinary art of Québec* deserves a whole chapter of its own. For centuries the province has been the culinary core of Canada. The immigrants from Normandy and Brittany, who were mostly simple fishermen and farmers, brought their recipes to the New World. Due to a lack of ingredients they often had to modify their recipes. Instead of pork, beef or chicken, they used *moose, deer, wild turkey or goose*. From the Native Americans they learned how to prepare corn and pumpkins, and instead of using sugar they sweetened their food with rich maple syrup.

Along the Atlantic, *lobster, fish and shellfish* are on the menu. The lobster – which grows very slowly in the cold Atlantic – is considered by connoisseurs

Photo: Distillery Historic District in Toronto

Canada's culinary charm is found in the diversity of the regional ingredients and recipes that were brought here by the immigrants

as the best in the world. On Prince Edward Island massive lobster buffets are served at lobster suppers which are held during the summer in community and church halls. The Scottish immigrants brought their porridge to Nova Scotia as well as the recipe for *Solomon Gundy*, delicious marinated herring. Some other traditional recipes from Newfoundland however, take some getting used to – for example fried cod tongues. Better known, and always good and fresh, is the calamari which is increasingly being fished off the coast of Newfoundland.

Further in the interior, in Ontario, the Niagara Peninsula, blessed with a mild climate, provides *fresh vegetables, wine and excellent fruit*. From the lakes in the hinterland, pike, whitefish and perch are often served together with wild rice, which the Native Americans harvest from the lakes of the north.

Your best bet for *breakfast* is in a coffee shop. Some of them are part of the hotel or are situated close to the motels. You

LOCAL SPECIALITIES

bagel with lox – iconic bun with smoked salmon and cream cheese (photo right)

bannock – Scottish flat bread baked in a pan (adapted by Native Americans as fry bread)

beavertail – fried pastry dusted with cinnamon and sugar

Caesar salad – Salad with parmesan anchovi dressing

caribou – strong red wine punch, very popular during the winter carnival

clam/seafood chowder – hearty cream-based mussel/fish soup

cipaille/cipate –traditional Québec dish, a layered meat pie with different types of meat

filet mignon – Filetsteak

hash browns – finely grated potatoes that are pan fried

lobster roll – Sandwich with lobster

Malpeque oysters – oysters from the Malpeque Bay on P.E.I.

onion rings – crispy fried onion rings

pancakes (flapjacks) – with maple syrup (photo left)

pickerel – freshwater fish widely found in Ontario

poutine – potato chips topped with curd cheese cubes and doused with gravy

pumpkin pie

scallops

sirloin steak

Solomon Gundy – marinated herring from Nova Scotia

soupe aux pois – hearty pea soup

summer sausage – spicy salami from the Mennonites in Ontario

tarte aux bleuets – blueberry pie

tourtière – deep-dish pie made with potatoes and various kinds of meat

turkey – with stuffing and gravy, yams and cranberry sauce

can either enjoy a small continental breakfast or order a large American breakfast with eggs and fried potatoes. Coffee is filled up free of charge. This is often really weak, but you can order a cappuccino or latte instead. You will only find stronger brewed Americano coffee in Quebec.

For *lunch*, between noon and 2pm, Canadians eat smaller dishes, which are listed on a separate lunch menu, usually a simple salad or soup and sandwich.

In the rural regions, *dinner* is served early between 5.30pm and 7pm, in the larger cities between 7pm and 10pm. In most restaurants you will need to *wait to be shown to your table*.

After dinner the final amount of the bill may not be what you anticipated: the prices shown on the menu do not include the *tax, which differs from province to province* and it is only shown on the bill. The tip is also usually not included; if you are happy with the service, a 15–18 per cent tip is the norm.

If there is a national drink in Canada, then it is *beer – aromatic and very palatable* especially when compared to the rather watery American beer – which goes well with a hearty steak. Everywhere in the country you will find *Molson Canadian* or *Labatt's Blue*, while speciality beers such as *Moosehead* are served only in some regions. Wine is served in most restaurants, while in the smaller restaurants in Québec that do not have an alcohol licence, you can bring your own. Good wines from California or France are often on the menu, but it is definitely worthwhile to try the *local wine* from Nova Scotia or from the Niagara Peninsula. If you like stronger drinks, you can rely on the excellent *Canadian whiskey*, which is either served on the rocks or – just like rum or gin – in mixed drinks.

Apart from the hotel bars, there are also many rustic pubs with pool tables and long bar counters. This is the best place to meet locals. Popular meeting places that are currently sprouting up are the *micro breweries*, which often have attached pubs. There are some excellent ales, wheat beer and other craft beers available.

A popular tradition that you will experience in Newfoundland is the *screech-in*. If it is your first time on the island, you

Lobster is a classic, especially in the Atlantic provinces

will hardly be able to escape it. Be it in private or in a bar, the ritual is always the same: the island newcomer has to put on the typical rain hat of the islanders, kiss a freshly caught cod (or any other large fish) and then drink a glass of pure, high-alcohol Newfoundland rum. Then you are an honorary Newfoundlander.

SHOPPING

The Canadian dollar is significantly weaker than the US dollar, but the converted prices are usually similar to those in Europe. Nevertheless, there are some bargains to be had: casual and sports wear, as well as vitamin pills and some food specialities, are cheaper in Canada than many other countries. You can also discover real gems at the frequent sales.

In the cities the supply is excellent; the variety of shops is just like Europe or the United States. In the hinterland however the variety of shopping possibilities decreases dramatically. A small grocery store that also sells shoes and chainsaws, or a gas station with a few shelves of items has to suffice in the little towns of the north. Thus, it is best to fully stock your camper with groceries and equipment before you leave town and embark on a long trip across country.

ARTS & CRAFTS

In Canada, arts and crafts are in high demand and most places have a craft fair for one or more weekends during the summer. There you can find turned wooden bowls, glass art, quirky ceram-ics or appealing watercolour paintings. St-Jean-Port-Joli in Québec is entirely dedicated to wood carving and sculpture – the craft capital of the New World. The crafts shops in the Atlantic provinces are also very good: here you find sailing accessories for yacht lovers, knitted pullovers from Newfoundland or jewellery made from Labradorite, a shiny blue stone that is only found in Labrador.

Also popular is the Irish-Celtic music of the immigrants, which is still maintained nowadays by modern artists such as Ashley MacIsaac or by the tap dance group Leahy, whose CDs are widely available.

CULINARY

The most famous souvenir from Canada is maple syrup. The thickened sap from maple trees usually comes from the deciduous forests of Québec and is an essential part of a hearty pancake breakfast in Canada. The crystallised sugar from the syrup is used in chocolates and biscuits. Other products are also tasty souvenirs, including wine from the Niagara Peninsula (the ice wine has become especially popu-

Shop until you drop, but only in the cities – in the hinterland the selection of goods and stores is limited

lar), blueberry jelly from Lac St-Jean, honey from the Île d'Orléans, lobster or smoked salmon from the Atlantic or pure beef summer sausages from the Mennonites in Kitchener.

MALLS & MARKETS

Shopping malls, departments stores and boutiques are to be found everywhere in the major cities. In Toronto the *Eaton Centre* and the exclusive shopping district of *Yorkville* are popular; in Montréal the *Rue Ste-Catherine* is the main shopping street. In some places the Canadians have built massive shopping complexes to escape the bitterly cold winter – such as the *Ville Souterraine* in Montréal with more than 30 km/18.6 mi of underground passages connecting approximately 2000 shops.

In the last decades, the old harbour waterfront districts are being renovated: in Halifax you have the restored *Historic Properties* area or Toronto's *Waterfront*, the chic shopping district around Queens Quay. In the major cities, colourful market streets of the immigrants such as the *Kensington Market* in Toronto or the *Boulevard St-Laurent* in Montréal attract many visitors.

NATIVE AMERICAN ART

Using ancient traditions, the Algonquin, Iroquois and the Ojibwa tribes produce baskets decorated with porcupine quills, beaded leather jackets and moccasins from moose leather. Typical of the region are also the small boxes and baskets from moulded birch bark. The Inuit of the Arctic are famous for their soapstone sculptures, which are also sold in galleries in Montréal, Toronto and Ottawa (from about C$300). More affordable are the art prints, like the ones produced by the Inuit in Cape Dorset or Pangnirtung.

TORONTO

CITY WHERE TO START?
Central starting point is the **City Hall (37 B3)** *(ⅢⅢ h3)*. From there it is not far west to the Art Gallery of Ontario museum, to Chinatown and the vibrant and colourful Queen Street West. Feel like some serious shopping? Then head east to the Eaton Centre, where you will also find a large car park close to the Queen and Osgoode subway stations.

MAP ON P. 37
The immigrants saved Toronto (146 C5) *(ⅢⅢ E13)*. **Fifty years ago, the capital of Ontario was seen as a sleepy, boring, provincial city – white, Anglo-Saxon and Protestant.**

A wave of immigrants after World War II swelled the population to almost 6.2 million and transformed Toronto into a modern and lively global city. The centre is filled with the mirrored glass towers of high finance and international companies. Around it, a mosaic of several ethnic neighbourhoods extends – a colourful mixture that shows itself in the hustle and bustle of Chinatown, in the Portuguese markets, in the Greek tavernas as well as in the Caribbean clubs. Toronto is worthy of its Native American name, which means gathering place. Only about 30 per cent of the citizens are of Anglo-Saxon origin.

Number one in the country: the metropolis on Lake Ontario is the booming economic centre of Canada

Trade and business flourished in Toronto from the 19th century. Yet it always played second fiddle to Montréal. It was only after World War II that Toronto gained ground: the St Lawrence Seaway was completed in 1959 and cargo ships travelled into the port of Toronto, immigrants streamed into the city and many companies have moved from Montréal to Toronto during the 1970s – after the threats of secession by the Québecers. During the 1980s Toronto overtook Montréal in population size and became the most important city in Canada, the engine of the entire country. A good 20 per cent of wares produced in Canada come from Toronto.

Toronto is also the city of culture. The national ballets, opera, as well as the *Toronto Symphony Orchestra* have their home here. Despite its size, Toronto is surprisingly clean and safe compared to the major American cities. And the quality of the air is the best among the world's major cities.

INSIDER TIP ► AGA KHAN MUSEUM
(146 C5) (*Ø E13*)

This museum is located at the Eastern edge of the city, yet it is a real treat for those who love the arts: the museum houses a unique collection of Islamic art and is housed in a super modern building that was created in 2014 by the Japanese architect Fumihiko Maki. *Tue–Sun 10am–6pm, Wed till 8pm | admission C$20 | 77 Wynford Dr. | www.agakhanmuseum.org*

tions. *Tue–Thu 10.30am–5pm, Wed, Fri 10.30am–9pm, Sat/Sun 10am–5.30pm | admission C$19.50 | 317 Dundas St. W | www.ago.ca*

BATA SHOE MUSEUM
(146 C5) (*Ø E13*)

The museum is housed in an appropriate form: a shoe box contains the only shoe museum in the whole of North America. You can see every type of footwear from ancient Egyptian sandals to Elton John's show boots. *Mon–Sat 10am–5pm,*

Not only winged shoes ... the Bata Shoe Museum has more than 12,000 pairs

ART GALLERY OF ONTARIO
(37 A3) (*Ø g3*)

One of the best and largest art museums in Canada gained an extension by star architect Frank Gehry in 2008. Especially worth seeing: the collection of around 900 works in the *Henry Moore Sculpture Centre*. The private collections include works by old masters such as Rembrandt and Tintoretto as well as European impressionists and surrealists, sculptures and Inuit prints to contemporary Canadian artists. All of this is supplemented by major touring exhibi-

Sun noon–5pm, Thu till 8pm | admission C$14 | 327 Bloor St. W | www.batashoe museum.ca

BAY STREET (37 A–C 1–4) (*Ø g–j 1–4*)

In the heart of the city, between Queen and Front Streets you will find the 'Wall Street' of Canada, with the modern office towers of the banks and the large corporations. The *Royal Bank* on the corner of Wellington Street shows its wealth: in both of the office towers, more than 2500 ounces of gold have been melted into the mirrored windows.

The most conspicuous building of the financial district is opposite: *Brookfield Place* topped by two towers with 49 and 53 floors, the *Galleria*, designed by the Spanish architect Santiago Calatrava which unites historic elements with avant-garde design.

THE BEACHES (146 C5) (*ʘ E13*)

This is a laid-back, young beach and residential district with a promenade on the lake shore. You can find good boutiques and restaurants that are situated in *Queen Street E. Tram 501*

CHINATOWN (37 A3) (*ʘ g3*)

Around the intersection of Dundas Street and Spadina Avenue you will find the best Chinese, Thai and Vietnamese restaurants and exotic shops.

CN TOWER ★ ☼ (37 B4) (*ʘ h4*)

After it was built in 1975 it remained the highest free-standing tower in the world for 30 years. Today there are several taller towers in Tokyo and Canton.

However, the view over Toronto and miles out into the surrounding area is terrific. The top observation deck (indoors) is at a height of 447 m/1467 ft while the open-air terrace with glass floor is situated at 342 m/1122 ft. One floor up you can enjoy the view from the revolving restaurant.

Guaranteed a unique experience for all adrenaline junkies and a real test of courage is the INSIDER TIP *EdgeWalk:* at a height of 356 m/1168 ft you can free walk around the tower on a broad ledge – with safety rope attached of course. There is also a flight simulator at the foot of the tower. *301 Front St. W | daily 8.30am–10.30pm | admission C$36, EdgeWalk C$225 | www.cn tower.ca*

Right next to the CN Tower, the *Rogers Centre*, the home stadium of the baseball team Blue Jays, rises up; it can seat 60,000 spectators and the roof, which weighs 11 000 tons, can open and close in just 20 minutes. *Daily guided tours | admission C$16 | 1 Blue Jays Way | info tel. 416 3 41 27 71 | www.cntower.ca*

★ CN Tower

A fantastic view over Toronto from one of the highest towers in the world – also a revolving restaurant → p. 35

★ Hockey Hall of Fame

The ultimate attraction for ice hockey fans is in the centre of Toronto → p. 36

★ Royal Ontario Museum

Spectacular architecture by Daniel Libeskind and some significant collections – everything from Egyptian mummies to Native American art → p. 38

★ Eaton Centre

Ideal for a spending spree: Toronto's massive shopping centre with 350 shops → p. 41

★ St Lawrence Market

Every Saturday, an unbelievable array of fresh meat, fish, cheese, fruits and vegetables – and Ontario's speciality: bacon on a bun → p. 41

★ St Jacobs

Journey back in time in the land of the Mennonites – just an hour west of Toronto you still see horse-drawn carriages → p. 43

MARCO POLO HIGHLIGHTS

DISTILLERY HISTORIC DISTRICT
(146 C5) (*E13*)

Today the old distillery in the east of the city centre is a monument to industrial history. Coffee shops and galleries now occupy the old brick buildings. The photos, caps and team uniforms in the *Sport Gallery* are well worth a visit. Festivals often take place here on weekends during the summer. *55 Mill St. | www.thedistill erydistrict.com*

FORT YORK (37 A5) (*g5*)

In the military fort built in 1793, soldiers in original uniforms illustrate the way of life in the former garrison. *In summer daily 10am–5pm, otherwise 10am–4pm, weekends until 5pm | admission C$14 | 250 Fort York Blvd.*

HARBOURFRONT
(37 B–C 4–5) (*h–j 4–5*)

Toronto's 'waterfront' was for many years a neglected area of the city. However, during the last few decades the piers along Lake Ontario have been given a new life. Marinas and shopping complexes have been developed, and during the past few years new glass apartment towers have shot up. Along Queens Quay boats depart for harbour cruises and cafés invite you to linger. In the INSIDER TIP *York Quay Centre* young artists show their talent in workshops and galleries, e.g. the highly dedicated ● *Power Plant Gallery*. It's no wonder then that half of Toronto seems to be strolling between *Queen's Quay Terminal* and *Pier 4* on weekends. *www. harbourfrontcentre.com*

HOCKEY HALL OF FAME ★
(37 C3) (*j3*)

Everything about the sport: exhibitions about the ice legend Wayne Gretzky, jerseys from all over the world, details on Canada's Olympic triumph and interactive exhibitions. Also the legendary *Stanley Cup,* Canada's most important trophy. *Mon–Sat 9.30am–6pm, Sun*

Always fascinating also from the water: the Toronto skyline

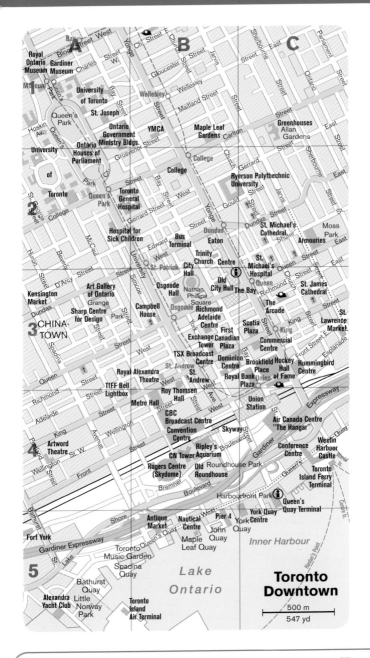

Toronto Downtown

500 m
547 yd

10am–6pm | admission C$19 | Brookfield Place | 30 Yonge St. | www.hhof.com

MUSEUM OF CONTEMPORARY CANADIAN ART (MOCCA) (146 C5) *(ᗰ E13)*

Expectations are high: there are plans for the MOCCA to move into new premises in the autumn of 2022. The museum will be located in the trendy quarter of Triangle west of the city where a few avant garde galleries displaying works by Canadian artists have already opened in former industrial buildings and car repair garages. *158 Sterling Rd. | www.museumofcontemporaryart.ca*

NATHAN PHILLIPS SQUARE (37 B3) *(ᗰ h3)*

This urban plaza is the heart of the city; the forecourt includes fountains and the *New City Hall* and was designed by the Finnish architect Viljo Revell in 1965. On the eastern side it borders the *Old Town Hall* from 1899 and the chic *Eaton Centre*. *Queen Street* runs in front of the square to the west while *Yonge Street,* with numerous shops and restaurants, runs behind Eaton Centre to the north.

PATH (37 B–C3) *(ᗰ h–j3)*

The perfect place for shoppers during bad weather: a 30 km/18.6 mi network of pedestrian tunnels, shopping arcades and malls that connect many of the larger buildings in the city centre.

QUEEN STREET, WEST (37 A3) *(ᗰ g3)*

At weekends, all hell breaks loose here: Queen Street west of the City Hall Is lined with chic boutiques and fashionable restaurants and bars. Beyond Spadina Avenue, there are numerous art galleries, second hand shops and design ateliers. Do not miss the crazy wall murals in the side streets around *Graffiti Alley (Rush Lane).*

RIPLEY'S AQUARIUM (37 B4) *(ᗰ h4)*

Sharks, rays, jellyfish and a total of 16,000 marine animals in a giant exhibition – including a nearly 100 m/328 ft long glass tunnel through the shark tank. *Daily 9am–11pm | admission C$33 | 288 Bremner Blvd. | www.ripleyaquariums.com*

ROYAL ONTARIO MUSEUM ★ ● (37 A1) *(ᗰ g1)*

In 2007, Canada's largest museum received a noteworthy architectural accent: Daniel Libeskind, the Polish-American architect, artist, professor and set designer of Polish-Jewish descent, designed the extension that rises up like a sparkling crystal. Inside is an incredible scientific collection: dinosaur skeletons, Egyptian mummies, Chinese temple art and Native American embroidery. Large special exhibitions are also often organised. Across the way is the *George R Gardiner Museum of Ceramic Art* with an excel-

The water basin on the Nathan Phillips Square transforms into an ice rink in winter

lent collection of majolica and Meissen porcelain. *Sat–Thu 10am–5.30pm, Fri 10am–8.30pm | admission C$16 | 100 Queen's Park | www.rom.on.ca*

TMX BROADCAST CENTRE
(37 B3) *(ⓜ h3)*

Canada's most important stock exchange only exists virtually – it is nothing but a large network of computers. The only thing real about it all is this futuristic visitor's centre that houses television studios, broadcasting information about the stock market. *In summer usually Mon–Fri 9am–5pm | admission free| Exchange Tower | King St. W | www.tmx.com*

INSIDER TIP TORONTO ISLANDS ☆
(146 C5) *(ⓜ E13)*

The small island group around 3 km/ 1.9 mi from the harbour front on Lake Ontario offer a fantastic view of Toronto's skyline in addition to parks, a small amusement park for kids, cafés, cycling paths (bicycles for hire) and beaches.
Ferry service from the beginning of Bay St. | www.torontoisland.com

TORONTO MUSIC GARDEN ●
(37 A–B5) *(ⓜ g–h5)*

In 1999 the famous cellist Yo-Yo Ma collaborated with a landscape designer to establish this unique garden on the waterfront – inspired by Bach's Cello Suite No. 1 in G Major. There are often concerts in summer. *Admission free | 475 Queens Quay W, between Bathurst St. and Spadina St.*

FOOD & DRINK

CANOE ☆ (37 A4) *(ⓜ g4)*

Elegant and expensive: new Canadian haute cuisine overlooking the skyscrapers from the 54th floor of the TD Bank. Slightly cheaper lunch menu.

66 Wellington St. W | tel. 416 3 64 00 54 | *Expensive*

EL CABALLITO (37 B3) (*ωω h3*)
Delicious Mexican food with freshly made guacamole and great margaritas. Excellent gourmet Mexican restaurant upstairs. *220 King St. W | tel. 416 6 28 98 38 | Moderate*

G FOR GELATO (37 C3) (*ωω j3*)
For all fans of Italian ice cream creations: greatly innovative flavours as well as tasty *panini*. Yummy! *75 Jarvis St. | tel. 416 7 92 17 61 | Budget*

LOW BUDGET

What's on Tonight sells tickets and much reduced remainder tickets for concerts, musicals and theatre performances for the same evening. Students can usually purchase tickets for C$5. Ticket sales via the app whatsontonight.ca

The most beautiful view of the skyline costs under C$8 – the price of a ticket on the *Toronto Island Ferry* to the small islands off the city.

Once a week the large museums of Toronto offer a discount: the *Art Gallery of Ontario* is free on Wednesday 6pm–9pm, and the *Royal Ontario Museum* 5.30pm–9pm is half price on Fridays.

With the *Citypass* coupon ticket you can visit five of the city's popular attractions for C$61.30 (almost 40 per cent discount), among them CN Tower, the *Ripley's Aquarium* and the *Royal Ontario Museum*.

THE KEG (37 B3) (*ωω h3*)
Chic steak restaurant serving prime meat from Alberta, with a large bar where a lot of young business people hang out after work. *165 York St. | tel. 416 7 03 17 73 | Moderate–Expensive*

KIT KAT (37 B3–4) (*ωω h3–4*)
Quirky Italian restaurant with an attractive courtyard. *297 King St. W | tel. 416 9 77 44 61 | Moderate*

INSIDER TIP MARS (146 C5) (*ωω E13*)
Eggs, griddle cakes, hamburgers: an iconic diner that has been offering the best and cheapest coffee shop food in the city since 1951. Most dishes cost under C$10. Breakfast around the clock. *432 College St. | tel. 921 63 32 | Budget*

INSIDER TIP PANTHEON
(146 C5) (*ωω E13*)
Souvlaki and moussaka in the middle of the Greek district, which is also popular for a stroll at night. *407 Danforth Ave. | tel. 416 7 78 19 29 | Budget*

REDS (37 B3) (*ωω h3*)
Chic bistro in the entertainment district with a very good selection of wines. *77 Adelaide St. W | tel. 416 8 62 73 37 | Budget–Moderate*

RODNEY'S OYSTER HOUSE
(37 A4) (*ωω g4*)
Rustic vaulted cellar with a fish market and lively restaurant. Speciality: oysters and lobster. Terrace above in the courtyard. *469 King St. W | tel. 416 3 63 81 05 | Moderate*

SHOPPING

Bloor, Yonge and *Queen Street* are the main shopping streets. Elegant shops can be found in *Yorkville* while the multicultural *Kensington Market (Kensington Ave, north of Dundas St.)* area has lots of colourful and eclectic shops and cafes.

EATON CENTRE ⭐ (37 B2) (*🛱 h2*)

The most beautiful temple of commerce in the city: a three-storey mall with approximately 350 shops, two department stores and a snow goose sculpture by Michael Snow. *Yonge St., between Dundas St. and Queen St. | www.torontoeaton centre.com*

ST LAWRENCE MARKET ⭐
(37 C3) (*🛱 j3*)

Since 1803 there has been a market held here every Saturday. The butchers, fish mongers and bakeries in the southern part of the building are also open on weekdays – and bacon on a bun in the *Carousel Bakery* is a tradition here. *Front St./Jarvis St.*

ENTERTAINMENT

You can enjoy concerts in the *Roy Thomson Hall (tel. 416 8 72 42 55)*, opera and ballet performances in the city's new opera house, the *Four Seasons Centre, (ticket sales from 11am on the day of the performance | 145 Queen St. W | tel. 416 3 63 82 31)*. In the beautifully renovated theatres of the theatre district you can catch top quality West End and Broadway musicals. Chic *Yorkville, King Street* and especially *Queen Street* are popular among bar goers and music fans. The rooftop bar of the *Thompson Hotel (550 Wellington St. W)* and the *Bar Raval (505 College St.)* inspired by Art Nouveau and Gaudí in Little Italy are both well worth visiting for a drink.

To watch some sports with a beer in hand, then try the INSIDER TIP huge sports bar *Real Sports (15 York St.)*. For dancing visit *The Fifth Social Club (225 Richmond St.*

The place to go for gourmets: St Lawrence Market

W) and the gay venue known for its drag shows INSIDER TIP *Crews and Tangos (508 Church St.)*. Jazz is played at the *Rex Bar (194 Queen St.)*, salsa at the *Lula Lounge (1585 Dundas St. W, with dance classes)*, acid rock and punk at the *Bovine Sex Club* bar *(542 Queen St.)*, funky music at the fusion Thai bar, pool hall and restaurant *Rivoli (334 Queen St. W)*, where Amy Winehouse ordered pad thai noodles. Then there is classic rock at the *Horseshoe Tavern (370 Queen St. W)*.

WHERE TO STAY

THE DRAKE (146 C5) *(ⓜ E13)*
Eclectic avant-garde hotel with night club and sushi bar. *19 rooms | 1150 Queen St. W | tel. 416 5 31 50 42 | www.thedrake hotel.ca | Moderate–Expensive*

FAIRMONT ROYAL YORK
(37 B–C4) *(ⓜ h–j4)*
This splendid, renovated castle hotel in the city centre was opened in 1929 and retains original features such as hand-painted ceilings. *1365 rooms | 100 Front St. W | tel. 416 3 68 25 11 | www.fairmont.com/royal-york-toronto | Moderate–Expensive*

HOTEL VICTORIA (37 C3) *(ⓜ j3)*
Older, but renovated and in the heart of the city. *56 rooms | 56 Yonge St. | tel. 416 3 63 16 66 | www.hotelvictoria-toronto. com | Budget–Moderate*

MADISON MANOR (146 C5) *(ⓜ E13)*
B & B situated in a Victorian villa right in the university district. It is located next to a pub and subway. *23 rooms | 20 Madison Ave. | tel. 416 9 22 55 79 | madisonmanorboutiquehotel.com | Budget–Moderate*

TEMPLAR HOTEL (37 A3–4) *(ⓜ g3–4)*
A smart, small design hotel just a few steps from the trendy Queen West area. *27 rooms | 348 Adelaide St. W | tel. 416 4 79 08 47 | www.templarhotel.com | Expensive*

INFORMATION

TORONTO VISITORS ASSOCIATION
(37 C4) *(ⓜ j4)*
Info stand in Union Station | 65 Front St. W | tel. 416 3 92 93 00 and 416 2 03 25 00 | www.seetorontonow.com

WHERE TO GO

KITCHENER-WATERLOO
(146 B5) *(ⓜ E13)*
The twin cities (pop. 525,000), 120 km/ 75 mi from Toronto, have been a stronghold of German settlers in Canada for over 100 years. S*chnitzel* and *sauerkraut*

MENNONITES: AN OLD-FASHIONED LIFE

Internet and telephone are taboo as are cars and even tractors! In the Mennonite country around Kitchener, you will see horse-drawn carriages being driven down the highway and farms with no access to electricity. They are farmers, deeply religious and sceptical about anything new (because the Bible has no reference to telephones or cars), living according to the old Christian ideals. Their ancestors came to Canada from Germany and Switzerland, Russia and the United States during the 19th century. Here they found the freedom to live according to their beliefs. As in the old days, the women work in the kitchen and help in the fields, the men plough and harvest with horse drawn wagons and scythes. You will find them at the markets and will hear them speaking in an old, dated form of German. There are about 300,000 Mennonites in Canada today, some of them do drive cars and are not as conservative as the *Old Order Mennonites* in their ancestral lands around Kitchener.

Travelling through the countryside at the speed of 1 HP – Mennonites don't need cars

is on many menus. Maypoles and *glock-enspiels* decorate the main streets, while the farmer's market offers sausages and black bread. The bustling city – housing many insurance company headquarters – does not hide its background. Up until WW I, Kitchener was called Berlin. English is the main language, yet every autumn the descendants of the immigrants remember their German roots and celebrate a big Oktoberfest.

The farmland north of Kitchener shows the very different lifestyle of the German pioneers. Deeply religious Mennonites live here. Between Heidelberg, Elmira and Elora you see them riding along the highway in old-fashioned horse-drawn carriages.

In ★ St Jacobs the visitor centre highlights their religion. On the farmer's market *(in summer Tue, Thu and Sat | Hwy. 85, Exit Rd. 15)* families sell vegetables, jams and very good sausages.

In the *Stone Crock Restaurant (1396 King St. N | tel. 519 6 64 22 86 | Moderate)*, traditional German food is served ranging from smoked sausage, schnitzel and sauerkraut. The adjoining bakery offers delicious pies.

MCMICHAEL CANADIAN ART COLLECTION (146 C4) (ω E13)

The museum, set in 100 acres of park at Kleinburg (approx. 40 km/24.9 mi north of Toronto), shows native art and Canadian paintings, incl. landscapes by the *Group of Seven. Daily 10am–5pm, in winter Tue–Sun 10am–4pm | admission C$18 | 10365 Islington Ave. | Kleinburg | www.mcmichael.com*

ONTARIO

Ontario – sparkling water. **This is the name that the Native Americans gave to the massive region, which extends between the Great Lakes and Hudson Bay. Ontario is definitely a water-shaped holiday destination with its old forts on the former canoe routes of the fur traders, its fine sandy beaches on the shores of Lake Ontario, Lake Erie and Lake Huron and of course the world-famous Niagara Falls.**

Ontario, with an area of approximately 415,000 mi², is the second largest province in Canada (after Québec) and is at the same time the richest region in the country. Massive deposits of mineral resources lie in the hard rock of the Canadian Shield to the north while in the mild, sunny climate in the south, agri-culture, fruit orchards and vineyards flourish. The vast majority of about 14 million inhabitants (more than one third of the total population) live .in the south of the province, especially in the greater metropolitan Toronto and Hamilton on the western edge of Lake Ontario. The vast, scarcely populated north remains the domain of loggers and miners, hunters and fishermen.

The Ontarians are mostly descendants of British immigrants, but in the east of the province live also many French Canadians. A number of Germans settled around Kitchener which is why today it is an area of contrasts, centre of the computer industry while at the same time the Mennonites live on their farms as their ancestors did 150 years ago.

Land of a thousand lakes: charming cities and interesting culture, scenic wilderness and forests – Ontario has it all

ALGONQUIN PROV. PARK

(146–147 C–D3) *(⨜ F11–12)* ★ ● **Canoeists and hikers are able to look forward to the oldest nature reserve in Ontario, which is a 2934 mi² mixture of forests and lakes that are home to moose, black bears and beavers.**

The park is very accessible, with numerous short nature trails leading off Hwy. 60

(which runs through it) through the typical forest vegetation. 1600 km/994 mi of canoe routes lead into the isolated hinterland. The visitor centre on Hwy. 60 includes a museum and provides maps for the tours. Canoe and equipment hire (also guided tours) at *Algonquin Outfitters (Oxtongue Lake | Dwight | tel. 800 4 69 49 48 | www.algonquinoutfitters.com)*.

Arowhon Pines is a large holiday lodge with log cabins on the lake in the middle of the park *(50 rooms | Algonquin Park | tel. 705 6 33 56 61, 416 4 83 43 93 | www.*

arowhonpines.ca | Expensive). ✳️ *Lake of Bays* has comfortable rooms and cabins overlooking the lake at the western entrance *(35 rooms| Dwight | tel. 705 6 35 38 38 | www.thelakeofbayslodge. com | Moderate)*.

home to several colleges – including the prestigious Queen's University.
The city, founded in 1673 as a fur trading post where the St Lawrence River flows from Lake Ontario, preserves its history despite the relatively young population.

Changing of the guard at Fort Henry, which was built as a defensive fortification

WHERE TO GO

INSIDER TIP ▶ HALIBURTON FOREST ❄️
(147 D3) (ⓜ F12)
At the southern edge of Algonquin Park, about 2 hours drive from the western entrance, is a fascinating eco centre, wolf enclosure and an educational trail in the treetops. Also camping and canoe rentals. *In summer daily 8am–5pm | admission C$16 | www.haliburtonforest.com*

KINGSTON

(147 D3) (ⓜ G13) Many young people live in the old garrison town (pop. 170,000) with its large marina, as it is

The typical blue-grey limestone was used for the construction of many historic buildings, which is how Kingston got its fitting nickname 'Limestone City'.

INFORMATION

KINGSTON VISITORS BUREAU
209 Ontario St. | tel. 613 5 48 44 15 | www. visitkingston.ca

SIGHTSEEING

FORT HENRY ✳️
Cannons fire and soldiers in colourful uniforms drill in front of thick walls. History is re-enacted in the huge fortress above the St Lawrence River - daily at 3pm. The war

of 1812 is the theme of the military museum. *End of May–end of Sept 10am–5pm | admission C$20*

CANADA'S PENITENTIARY MUSEUM

The Penitentiary Museum is definitely a bit spooky: it owes its location here to the fact that Kingston has the most and largest penitentiaries in Canada. You can see old photos of cells and prison riots, tools and weapons used for breaking out and hear the stories of legendary prisoners. If you are lucky, you can take part in a guided tour given by retired prison guards. *Open 9am–6pm in the summer | Free entrance, donations requested | 555 King St. | www.penitentiarymuseum.ca*

TOURS

ISLAND QUEEN ※
Boat tours in the island labyrinth of the Thousand Islands. *Departure from Crawford Dock | tickets C$30–78 | tel. 613 5 49 55 44 | www.1000islandscruises.ca*

WHERE TO STAY

FRONTENAC CLUB INN
Well-maintained guest house in a former bank in the old town. *14 rooms | 225 King St. E | tel. 613 5 47 61 67 | www.frontenacclub.com | Moderate*

MANITOULIN ISLAND

(146 A3) *(፱ C–D11)* **Five Native American reservations are situated on the island (176 km/109 mi long) in Lake Huron, the largest island in a freshwater lake.**

In the small reservation towns you can buy woven grass baskets decorated with porcupine quills and other craft items by the *Ojibwa*. A large pow-wow is held in early August. For information about festivals, attractions and Native American tours in the region and good background information visit the *Great Spirit Circle Trail* website *(www.circletrail.com)*.

MIDLAND

(146 C4) *(፱ E12)* **A health resort (pop. 16,000) and water sports centre on the shore of the Georgian Bay. Here in the Hurons ancestral area, the Jesuits founded a mission in 1639 – with little success: eight missionaries died at the stake.**

The *Huronia Museum (in summer daily 9am–5pm, otherwise closed on Sat/Sun | admission C$12 | Little Lake Park)* has exhibits about the history of the Hurons and a replica Native American village.

⭐ *Sainte-Marie among the Hurons (in summer daily 10am–5pm | admission C$12 | Hwy. 12)* is a living museum and an impressive reconstruction of the Jesuit mission from 1639. Stay overnight in the beautiful Victorian house ⚫ *The Victorian Inn (3 rooms | 670 Hugel Ave. | tel. 705 5 26 44 41 | www.victorianinn.ca | Budget–Moderate)*.

LOW BUDGET

During the summer the *National Capital Commission* in Ottawa organises various ⚫ concerts and theatre performances in the parks – which are often free of charge. Information at *www.ncc. ccn.gc.ca*.

Discount shopping: not quite as cheap as in the United States, but in the *Canada One Factory Outlets (daily 10am–9pm, Sun in winter until 6pm | 7500 Lundy's Lane | Niagara Falls)* there are more than 40 firms to choose from. Another good option is the *St Jacobs Outlet Mall* in Kitchener.

Buy everything you need for a picnic in the *wine lands* on the Niagara Peninsula at affordable prices in *Hendriks Valu Mart (130 Queen St. | Niagara-on-the-Lake)*. Many vineyards have tables and seats for a picnic.

WHERE TO GO

GEORGIAN BAY ISLANDS ⚫
(146 C3–4) (⌖ E12)

The wildly romantic island group in the south-eastern Georgian Bay was made famous by the paintings of the *Group of Seven*. Boat tours and water taxis. *Departure in Midland with the excursion boat 'Miss Midland' (fare C$32 | tel. 705 5 49 33 88 | www.midlandtours.com)* and in Honey Harbour at the end of Hwy. 5.

WASAGA BEACH (146 C4) (⌖ E12)

Very popular holiday resort with a 14 km/8.7 mi long sandy beach, approx. 40 km/24.9 mi south-west of Midland. Water parks, mini golf, nice holiday motels – in short: summer beach fun.

NIAGARA FALLS

(146 C5) (⌖ E13) ⭐ ⚫ **The thundering waterfalls on the Niagara River, which connects Lake Erie with Lake Ontario, are without doubt one of the greatest natural wonders of North America, and one that is also marketed relentlessly.**
Since the first white man, the Jesuit missionary Louis Hennepin, saw the falls in 1678 much has changed. Two cities, both with the name *Niagara Falls,* are situated on either side of the river which forms the border between Canada and the United States. Between them the falls plunge down, surrounded by gardens and protected as a national park. All around is the tourist hustle and bustle that accompanies such attractions. Some take their names from the falls, such as the *Daredevil Exhibit* with its IMAX movie theatre, where you can experience

the falls cinematically. Others, how-ever, are just there to profit from the stream of tourists: neon exhibits, roller coasters, water parks and all sorts of souvenirs.

If you feel like escaping, it is a good option to take a ride on the ⚜ *Niagara Parkway,* a road that runs parallel to the river through green landscapes and past the *Botanical Gardens* to Lake Ontario in the north.

HORNBLOWER NIAGARA CRUISES

Boat tours to the foot of the thundering waterfalls are a wet, but amazing experience. *In summer daily, closed in winter due to ice | fare C$26 | departure at Clifton Hill St. | www.niagaracruises.com*

TABLE ROCK/NIAGARA'S FURY/JOURNEY BEHIND THE FALLS ⚜

At *Table Rock* at the Canadian end of the falls you can experience the immersive

Experiencing the Niagara Falls from the water is a must – the red rain cape apparently too

SIGHTSEEING

HORSESHOE/AMERICAN FALLS

The 54 m/177.2 ft high Canadian *Horse-shoe Falls* are much more impressive than the 56 m/183.7 ft high American Falls, which arc in a 670 m/2198 ft wide semi-circle. The most beautiful viewing spot on the Canadian side is at ⚜ *Table Rock House* and on the American side at *Luna Island*. Colourful illumination at night.

4-D experience 'Niagara's Fury' and also take a tunnel behind the falls to observation decks at the foot of the falls. *In summer 9am–10pm, otherwise until 5.30pm | group tickets including boat trip from C$57.*

FOOD & DRINK

BRAVO!

Perfect after a long sightseeing tour: great pizza and a huge beer selection. *5438 Ferry St. | tel. 905 3 54 33 54 | Moderate*

QUEENSTON HEIGHTS
Beautifully located terrace restaurant some 15 min drive downstream on the Niagara Parkway. Sunday brunch. *Queenston Heights Park | tel. 905 2 62 42 74 | Moderate*

SKYLON DINING ROOM ⚜
Revolving restaurant in the 160 m/525 ft high observation tower with panoramic views of the falls. *tel. 905 3 56 26 51 | Moderate*

SMOKE'S POUTINERIE
Here you should try: poutine (see p. 80), a typically Canadian fast food classic in the midst of the tourist hype. *5869 Victoria Ave. | tel. 905 3 56 28 73 | Moderate*

cuisine, most of their ingredients are from organic farmers in the region. View of the falls. *5875 Falls Ave. | tel. 866 3 74 44 08 | Expensive*

WHERE TO STAY

CLIFTON VICTORIA INN
A good mid-range hotel for families. Centrally located opposite a water park. *127 rooms | 5591 Victoria Ave. | tel. 905 3 57 16 26 | www.cliftonvictoriainnatthefalls.com | Budget–Moderate*

FOUR POINTS SHERATON ⚜
Top class, modern hotel overlooking the falls, in the centre of the tourist hubbub. There are 18 floors and the upper floor rooms have views of the falls.

Worthwhile: a trip to the lively town Niagara-on-the-Lake

WINDOWS ⚜ ⬛
For special occasions: elegant evening restaurant with gourmet Canadian

141 rooms | 6455 Fallsview Blvd. | tel. 905 3 57 52 00 | www.fourpointsniagarafallsview.com | Moderate–Expensive

INSIDER TIP SOUTH LANDING INN

A cosy country inn some miles downstream. *23 rooms | 21 Front St. S | Queenston | tel. 905 2 62 46 34 | www.south landinginn.ca | Moderate*

TRAVELODGE FALLSVIEW

A somewhat old building, but well renovated and offering a view of the falls. *130 rooms | 5599 River Rd. | tel. 905 3 54 27 27 | www.travelodge.ca | Expensive*

INFORMATION

NIAGARA FALLS VISITORS BUREAU

Large information centre in the Table Rock House at the falls and at 5400 Robinson St. | Niagara Falls | tel. 905 3 56 60 61 | www.niagarafallstourism.com

WHERE TO GO

LONG POINT (146 C5) (*∅ E13*)

About one hour's drive west of Niagara lies this sport, adventure and nature area with beautiful beaches. The highlight is a zipline with 12 cables, as well as canoe and bike tours and also luxury tents – in case you want to spend the night. *Long Point Eco-Adventures | 1730 Front Rd. | Turkey Point | tel. 877 7 43 86 87 | www.lpfun.ca*

NIAGARA-ON-THE-LAKE ★
(146 C5) (*∅ E13*)

Just the drive along the Niagara Parkway alone is worthwhile. The small town at the mouth of the Niagara River in Lake Ontario, about 15 km/9.3 mi north of the falls, delights with pretty, historic brick buildings and Victorian facades from the 19th century. The famous *Shaw Festival* runs here for the whole summer. ● Wine lovers who want to explore the various vineyards should stay over at the *Cape House B & B (3 rooms | 1895 Lakeshore Rd. | tel. 905 68 83 80 | www. capehouse bb.com | Moderate)*, a romantic, stylish guest house.

ST CATHARINES (146 C5) (*∅ E13*)

Grapes, peaches, strawberries and vegetables flourish in the mild climate of the Niagara Peninsula and in the middle of it lies St Catherines, almost 20 km/12.4 mi west of the Niagara falls. The town celebrates its agricultural production with several festivals in spring and autumn. At lock no. 3 on the Welland Canal you can watch the St Lawrence Seaway's extremely busy shipping traffic.

OTTAWA

MAP ON P. 52

(147 E3) (*∅ G12*) **Canada's capital (pop. 1.4 million) on the Ottawa River is famous for its lifestyle and excellent quality of life.**

Although it is the coldest capital – temperature-wise – in the Western world, it is also the cleanest. There are no air-polluting industries – Ottawa's only job is to govern the nation.

CITY WHERE TO START?
To the **parliament**: at 10am it is the changing of the guard in front. A good starting point with many attractions nearby: across the **Rideau Canal** and past the **Château Laurier** you will reach the **Nepean Point** for a lovely view of the city and the Ottawa River. Right next to it you will find the **National Art Gallery** and the lively old town district around the **Byward Market**. Parking: on York St. or in the car park of the George St./ Byward Market. bus 1, 2, 7, 9, 12

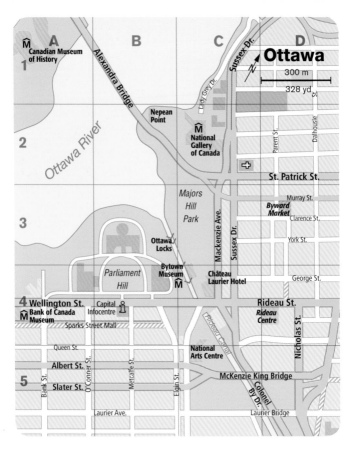

British traditions such as the ceremonial changing of the guards in front of parliament *(in summer, daily 10am)* have been retained as popular tourist events. However, the French lifestyle has spilt over the Ottawa River from Québec and changed the once sleepy capital into a tremendously vibrant metropolis.

There is no shortage of culture, they have a modern *National Arts Centre* with an opera house and museums for any area of interest. Afterwards you can relax in the cafés around the colourful *Byward Market* in the old town or in one of the many parks along the flower-lined *Rideau Canal,* which runs through the city centre and connects Ottawa to the city of Kingston on Lake Ontario.

SIGHTSEEING

BYWARD MARKET (52 D3)

The best place to experience the lifestyle of the city is in this district, established in 1826, with its market stalls, street cafés and trendy bars. Try Ottawa's speciality

INSIDER TIP *beavertails*, delicious fried dough pastry, right at the baker's stand. The best: *Killaloe Sunrise* – with lemon. *George St./Byward Market Square | www. byward-market.com*

CANADIAN MUSEUM OF HISTORY ★ (52 A1)

Spectacular architecture on the banks of the Ottawa River, where the curved forms and materials used emulate the landscapes and cultures of Canada. The museum was opened in 1989 – it is the most visited museum in the country – and houses excellent collections on Native American and Inuit cultures in Canada and on the frontier history. Interesting: the multi-storey high hall with totem poles. *Daily 9.30am–5pm, in summer until 6pm, Thu always until 8pm | admission C$20 | Gatineau | 100 Laurier St. | www.historymuseum.ca*

CANADIAN WAR MUSEUM (147 E3) (*⊞ G12*)

A spectacular new building on the Ottawa River – despite the name it also has good exhibitions of Canada's role in UN peacekeeping forces. *In summer daily 9.30am–6pm, Thu until 8pm, otherwise daily 9.30am–5pm | admission C$13 | 1 Vimy Place | www.warmuseum.ca*

NATIONAL GALLERY OF CANADA (52 C2)

Excellent Canadian and European art highlights in a building designed by Moshe Safdie. *In summer daily 9.30am–6pm, rest of the year Tue–Sun 9.30am–5pm, Thu always until 5pm | admission C$15 | 380 Sussex Dr.| www.gallery.ca*

PARLIAMENT HILL (52 B3–4)

The city's prominent position is taken up by Canada's parliament on a cliff on the southern banks of the Ottawa River.

Construction of the neo-Gothic *Parliament* began in 1859, just two years after Queen Victoria declared the remote lumberjack camp of *Bytown* the new capital, thus destroying the hopes of Montréal and Toronto. Within a few years it became a 'Westminster in the wilderness'. *In summer daily at 10am ceremonial changing of the guard and evening son et lumière shows | free guided tours* You will have the best views from ☼ *Nepean Point* behind the National Gallery, where Samuel de Champlain looks out

Native American and Inuit art in the Canadian Museum of History

The library next to the imposing Parliament almost appears to be a Gothic church

over the Ottawa River from a podium. He was the first white to travel here in 1613.

FOOD & DRINK

CANAL RITZ (147 E3) (*m G12*)

Somewhat outside of the centre, but in a beautiful setting on the ☆ *Rideau Canal*. Delicious mussels, salads and pasta. *375 Queen Elizabeth Dr. | tel. 613 2 38 89 98 | Moderate*

LUXE (52 D3)

Good steaks, a pleasant terrace and per-fectly situated close to Byward Market. *47 York St. | tel. 619 2 41 88 05 | Moderate*

PURE KITCHEN ⊘ (147 E3) (*m G12*)

Everything is organic and fresh in this fashionable vegetarian restaurant: soups and tasty sandwiches accompa-nied by fruit juices, gluten-free beer and delicious cocktails. *340 Elgin St. | tel. 613 2 33 78 73 | Budget–Moderate*

SHOPPING

The most attractive shopping district is the old town around the *Byward Market* with speciality stores and art galleries. The *Rideau Centre (corner of Rideau St./ Colonel By Dr.)* in the city centre has over 200 shops. In the pedestrian zone *Sparks Street Mall* small bookstores, galleries and boutiques are squeezed in next to each other.

TOURS

PAUL'S BOAT LINES ☆

Sightseeing trips on the Ottawa River and the Rideau Canal. *Departure:*

Ottawa Locks and Hulls Marina in Gatineau | tel. 613 2 25 67 81 | www.paulsboatline.com

ENTERTAINMENT

Experience theatre, ballet and concerts in the *National Arts Centre (info tel. 613 9 47 70 00 | www.nac-cna.ca)*. Popular meeting spots are the clubs and bars in the city centre such as *Pub 101 (101 York St.)* at the Byward Market, the country dance club *Great Canadian Cabin (95 York St.)* and the *Rainbow Bistro (76 Murray St.)*.

WHERE TO STAY

THE ALT (52 A5)

Very central location, in a cool industrial look design with amusing, functional designer furniture. *148 rooms | 185 Slater St. | tel. 613 6 91 68 82 | www.althotels. com | Moderate*

FAIRMONT CHÂTEAU LAURIER (52 C4)

Built in 1912, this castle style grand hotel – once the seat of the Prime Minister Sir Wilfrid Laurier – offers dignified luxury and a view of parliament. *429 rooms | 1 Rideau St. | tel. 613 2 41 14 14 | www.fairmont.com | Moderate–Expensive*

INSIDER**TIP** OTTAWA B & B NETWORK
Listings of half a dozen well-kept guesthouses such as the *Benner's* in the east of the city centre. *7 rooms | 541 Besserer St. | tel. 613 7 89 83 20 | www.bennersbnb. com | Budget–Moderate*

INFORMATION

OTTAWA TOURISM (52 B4)

Information centre 90 Wellington St. | tel. 800 3 63 44 65 | www.ottawatourism.ca, www.ncc-ccn.gc.ca

WHERE TO GO

MORRISBURG (147 E4) (*Ø G12*)

During the construction of the St. Lawrence Seaway, the entire village of Morrisburg (pop. 2500) was forced to move to the new higher bank of the river about one hour's drive south of Ottawa. The 35 old houses of the loyalist settlers were restored and rebuilt in the museum village *Upper Canada Village (in summer daily 9.30am–5pm | admission C$18 | www. uppercanadavillage.com)* on Highway 2. Experience everyday life in 1800: the farmers plough with oxen, yarn is spun in the living room. At the large gift shop you can buy Canadian crafts and reproduction items made by village artisans.

North of the village, a scenic road the ⚜ INSIDER**TIP** *Long Sault Parkway* leads past pretty swimming spots and viewing points that look out over the eleven islands in the St Lawrence.

PARC DE LA GATINEAU (147 E3)(*Ø G12*)

Bicycle lanes and ⚜ scenic roads crisscross the 130 mi² of this large park filled with forests and lakes on the northern shore of the Ottawa River right in front of the town's gates. The viewing spots are especially beautiful during autumn when the leaves start to change colour at the beginning of September. *Visitor centre in Chelsea | access from Hwy. 5*

POINT PELEE NAT. PARK

(146 A6) (*Ø C14*) **The southernmost point of Canada – situated on roughly the same latitude as Rome – is the best place for bird watching in Eastern Canada.**

Lake Erie – a favourite swimming spot for Canadians in the summer – has a 20 km/12.4 mi sandbank where tens of thousands of birds gather May and September. Another fantastic spectacle of nature are the INSIDER TIP swarms of monarch butterflies that fly thousands of miles from Mexico and arrive in mid-September. A tip for amateur ornithologists: take a day trip by boat to *Pelee Island*.

WHERE TO GO

DRESDEN (146 A5) (*Ø D13*)
The farming village (current pop. 2600) with a German name was a dream destination for slaves from the USA around 1850: The *Underground Railroad* ended there, the railroad was the secret escape route for slaves fleeing the southern United States.

One of the refugees was a certain Josiah Henson, whose life was apparently the model for the 1852 novel INSIDER TIP 'Uncle Tom's Cabin' by Harriet Beecher Stowe. Today Henson's house has been turned into an interesting literary museum *(Tue–Sat 10am–4pm, Sun noon–4pm | Park St. W | admission C$7 | www.uncletomscabin.org)* About an hour's drive north-east of the Point Pelee National Park.

SAULT SAINTE MARIE

(144 C6) (*Ø C10–11*) The industrial and harbour city (pop. 73,000) lies directly

A flock of ring-billed gulls flies up in Lake Erie on the National Park Point Pelee

at the border to the US, on the narrow point between Lake Superior and Lake Huron. It is a good starting point for tours to the hinterland, to the rugged coast of Lake Superior and to the fishful lakes.

The mighty rapids, where the Jesuits built a Native American mission in 1669, are circumvented by the St Lawrence Seaway's impressive *canal lock system (boat trips from the US-side)*. In the *Canadian Bushplane Heritage Centre (mid May–mid Oct 9am–6pm, otherwise 10am–4pm | admission C$12 | 50 Pim St. | www. bushplane.com)* you can view twenty historic aircraft and explore the era of bush flying. Especially lovely during the autumn are the day-long train excursions to the Agawa Canyon with the *Algoma Central Railway (129 Bay St. | tel. 705 9 46 73 00 | www.agawatrain. com). Information: Algoma Travel Association | 334 Bay St. | tel. 705 2 54 42 93 | www. algomacountry.com*

SUDBURY

(145 E5) (*∅ E11*) In the Sudbury Basin, compasses go wild, not pointing north, but instead down to the earth! This is due to the huge amount of metals underground, including nickel, copper, iron, silver and cobalt. It is said that the gigantic volume of ore deposits originated from a meteorite hitting the earth around 2 billion years ago.

That explains Sudbury's role as the most important mining town in northern Ontario (pop. 165,000). In the *Big Nickel Mine (in summer daily 9am–6pm | admission museum/mine C$35)*, which is part of the *Science North* museum complex, mining techniques are shown in the *Dynamic Earth* exhibit. INSIDER TIP ▶ A popular area for canoeists is the *Killar-*

ney Provincial Park (canoe rentals at the park entrance) on the banks of Georgian Bay, south of the city.

THUNDER BAY

(144 A4) (*∅ A9*) The city (pop. 120,000) on the north-western shore of Lake Superior lies in the centre of the continent and has the third largest harbour in Canada. Many of the massive grain silos in the harbour are now empty, the grain that came from the prairies and was shipped via the St Lawrence Seaway to the Atlantic 3700 km/2299 mi away, is now transported to the Pacific. In the *Centennial Park* on the Current River there are almost 30 km/18.6 mi of hiking and biking trails as well as exhibitions about logging.

SIGHTSEEING

OLD FORT WILLIAM ★

On the south-western outskirts is a reconstructed 1816 fur trading fort that re-creates the trapper days of the *North West Trading Company*. Experience the lifestyle of the Native Americans and trappers as you stroll around the 40 buildings of the former trading post. Gaze at the completely light-pollution-free night sky above the Thunder Bay from the adjoining *Astronomy Centre* and watch planets and galaxies. *In summer daily 10am–5pm | admission C$14 | Broadway Ave. | www.fwhp.ca*

INFORMATION

TOURISM THUNDER BAY

Terry Fox Centre | Hwy. 11–17 | tel. 800 6 67 83 86 | www.thunderbay.ca

MONTRÉAL

MAP INSIDE BACK COVER

WHERE TO START?
Start at the **PLACE JACQUES-CARTIER (U E3) (*∭ e3*)** in the heart of the winding old town, with the Basilique Notre-Dame and the bustling piers of the old harbour nearby. From here you can reach the Rue Ste-Catherine shopping thoroughfare, the Musée des Beaux-Arts or the trendy scene on the Rue St-Denis in the Plateau Mont-Royal district.

There is ample parking space on the Rue de la Commune, east of Place Jacques Cartier – or you can take a *Bixi* rental bike from your hotel.

Montréal (147 F3) (*∭ H12*) **is the second largest city in Canada with nearly 4.1 million citizens. And as the city has lots of sights and historical monuments, it needs to be explored and experienced.** There is ample parking space on the Rue de la Commune, east of Place Jacques Cartier – or you can take a *Bixi* rental bike from your hotel.

Only then will you experience the joie de vivre of the city's inhabitants and appreciate their diverse culture. In the summer, when life revolves around the street cafés and parks, the city is at its most enjoyable. Seventy per cent of Montréal speaks French, and the Gallic temperament – the enjoyment of good food and a chat in the bistro – is very much intact

A metropolis with Gallic charm: works of art, bistros, bars and elegant boutiques – in Montréal the old world meets the new

despite 250 years of British affiliation. Closing time is not until 3am and Montréalers take full advantage of this.

The city lies on the same latitude as Milan. But has neither the Mediterranean Sea nor the Alps to mitigate the climate. So the summers are hot and humid, while the winters are bitterly cold and snowy. The first French settlers had a rather tough reception when they founded the city in 1642. They had to deal with the warlike Iroquois who lived on the 50 km/31.1 mi long island in the St Lawrence. Peace was declared in 1701 and Montréal flourished as a settler centre and fur trading city.

From here the traders and travellers set forth into the forests of the west and the north, from where they conquered the continent. Montréal was the last port along the St Lawrence – the rapids above the settlement could not be crossed by sailors. Today these rapids are still called *Lachine*, because the discoverer Jacques Cartier believed that the rapids led to the Northwest Passage and to China. In the

19th century, Montréal quickly become Canada's most important city, but the Separatist crisis in the 1970s caused a severe recession. Many Anglo-Canadian companies left for the 'safer' Ontario.

ken. Running north-south through the city centre is the *Boulevard St-Laurent* which also divides the city's neighbourhoods with the English to the west, the French to the east on the *Rue St Denis*

Lights on! Lantern Festival in the huge Chinese garden of Jardin Botanique

The 1990s saw the beginning of a new boom – with people returning from Toronto to enjoy the French-Canadian lifestyle.

SIGHTSEEING

Orientation in Montréal is easy. On the southern banks of the Île de Montréal lies the old town *(Vieux Montréal)*, full of nooks and crannies and cobbled streets. Behind it are the skyscrapers of the city itself, gently sloping towards the river between the old town and Mount Royal. To the west of the city centre is the residential and shopping district of *Westmount,* where English is mostly spo-

and many of the immigrant communities in the middle. The old town and city centre can easily be explored on foot, and there is always a metro station nearby. And do not worry if you get lost, the friendly Montréalers will gladly help you get back on track.

INSIDER TIP ▶ **BARBIE EXPO** ●
(147 F3) (*ⓜ C4*)
Wonderfully crazy, but unique: 1000 Barbie dolls wearing designer clothing by Dior and Armani. This must be the largest Barbie exhibition in the whole world. *Open daily 10am–6pm, Sun midday–5pm | admission free | 1455, Rue Peel im Les Cours Mont-Royal*

BIODÔME ★ (147 F3) (*Ⓜ H12*)
The former *Parc Olympique* velodrome today houses an eco-museum that includes replicas of the four most important ecosystems of the American continent, including rain forests and Arctic ice caves. *In summer daily 9am–6pm, otherwise Tue–Sun 9am–5pm | admission C$20.25, with Jardin Botanique C$35 | 4777, Ave. Pierre de Coubertin | www.espacepourlavie.ca*

ÎLE STE-HÉLÈNE (147 F3) (*Ⓜ H12*)
The parks of the small island, which is situated in the St Lawrence River off the old town, are a popular recreation destination for Montréalers. There is the *La Ronde* amusement park and also an old fort, *Fort de Île Ste-Hélène* dating back to 1822 (with military museum), where soldiers in historical costumes parade during the summer. In the southern part of the island and on the neighbouring island *Île Notre-Dame* the Expo 67 took place. Some of the buildings that have been preserved include the former French pavilion with *casino* and the huge

INSIDER TIP *Biosphère (in summer daily 10am–5pm, in winter Thu/Tue closed | admission C$15 | www.ec.gc.ca/biosphere)* – once the United States pavilion – where you can view exhibitions on ecology, climate and water and air quality. Île Notre-Dame is also where Montréal's *Grand Prix* racing circuit is situated.

JARDIN BOTANIQUE (147 F3) (*Ⓜ H12*)
With 30 sections, Montréal's botanical garden ranks as one of the best in the world. There are Japanese and Indian gardens (fantastic bonsai trees!), as well as a fascinating insectarium, where you can admire over 4000 beetles, caterpillars, butterflies and spiders. *In summer daily 9am–6pm, otherwise Tue–Sun 9am–5pm | admission C$20.25 with Biodôme C$35 | 4101, Rue Sherbrooke Est*

MONT ROYAL (U A2–3) (*Ⓜ a2–3*)
The mountain that gave Montréal its name is today a 300 acre forested park. From the Mont Royal's *Grand Chalet* ★ ☖ *terrace* you will have fantastic views of the city skyline, and you can also reach

it on foot. The *Visitor centre (daily 9am–6pm | 1260 Remembrance Rd.)* in the *Smith House* in the centre of the park has a restaurant with a terrace that is ideal for a break.

MUSÉE D'ART CONTEMPORAIN
(U C–D3) *(𝄞 c–d3)*

Contemporary art, various Québec artists in an extensive spacious post-modern building. Good bookshop. *Tue 11am–6pm, Mon–Fri 11am–9pm, Sat/Son 10am–6pm | admission C$15 | 185, Rue Ste-Catherine Ouest | www.macm.org*

MUSÉE DES BEAUX-ARTS
(U B4) *(𝄞 b4)*

Canada's oldest art museum is famous for its large special exhibitions in the new building by the Canadian architect Moshe Safdie. Good museum shop. *Tue–Thu 10am–5pm, special exhibition Wed until 9pm | admission free for people up to an age of 30 years, otherwise C$15, special exhibition C$23, up to 30 years C$15 | 1380, Rue Sherbrooke Ouest | www.mbam.qc.ca*

MUSÉE MCCORD (U C3) *(𝄞 c3)*

A small, fine museum about the history of Canada that also has some wonderful Native American beadwork. *In summer daily 10am–6pm, Wed until 9pm, Sat/Sun until 5pm, during the winter closed on Mon | admission C$15 | 690, Rue Sherbrooke Ouest | www.mccord-museum.qc.ca*

L'ORATOIRE ST-JOSEPH
(147 F3) *(𝄞 H12)*

Québecers are strongly Catholic and this basilica is their place of pilgrimage. The church is dedicated to the miracle healer

Basilique Notre-Dame in Vieux Montréal is a neo-Gothic splendour that dates from 1843

Frère André. The massive dome of the basilica (97 m/318.2 ft high) is the second highest in the world after St Peter's. *Daily 7am–9pm, carillon Wed–Fri noon and 3pm, Sat/Sun noon and 2.30pm | 3800, Chemin Queen Mary*

PARC OLYMPIQUE ☀ (147 F3) (*⬚ H12*)

Rising above the 1976 Olympic stadium is the dramatic 165 m/541 ft inclined tower, one of the city's most popular attractions. The futuristic stadium's spectacular tower, with its 45 degree angle, was only completed eleven years after the Olympic Games following numerous construction scandals. The view from the observation deck is best in the morning and at night. *In summer daily 9am–8pm, Mon from 1pm, in winter until 5pm | admission C$23.25 | 4141, Ave. Pierre-de-Coubertin*

POINTE-À-CALLIÈRE ⭐ (U E4) (*⬚ e4*)

City history with a difference: after a spectacular multimedia introduction you can walk underneath the Place Royale in a subterranean labyrinth of old ruins, past the city's first cemetery, an early tavern and the foundations of the first settlers' fort. *Mon–Fri 10am–6pm, Sat/Sun 11am–6pm, otherwise Tue–Sun until 5pm | admission C$20 | 350, Place Royale | www.pacmusee.qc.ca*

RUE ST-DENIS (U C–E 1–2) (*⬚ c–e 1–2*)

Street cafés, cinemas and small restaurants characterise the area around the *Université du Québec.* North-west of this – at the intersection to the Avenue du Mont-Royal – the lively ⭐ *Plateau Mont-Royal* district starts. Today funky boutiques and bistros reside in the brick buildings of the former immigrants. Tip for refreshments: INSIDER TIP a bagel in the *St-Viateur* bakery *(1127, Ave du Mont-Royal Est | www.stviateurbagel.com).*

RUE STE-CATHERINE

(U A–E 6–1) (*⬚ a–e 6–1*)

Shopping, eating, looking: this is the main thoroughfare of the city centre. On the southern side of *Dorchester Square* (info centre) is the *Cathédrale Marie-Reine-du-Monde,* a smaller, but true to detail, version of St Peter's in Rome.

INSIDER TIP LA TOHU ◎

(147 F3) (*⬚ H12*)

A highlight for circus fans: a circus school and training centre for Cirque du Soleil was built to eco-friendly standards on what was once a rubbish dump. Often also very innovative circus performances: *daily 9am–5pm | 2345, Rue Jarry Est | tel. 514 3 76 86 48 | www.tohu.ca*

VIEUX MONTRÉAL (U D-E3) (*⬚ d–e3*)

The most important attractions of the old town lie around the Place Jacques Cartier and the Place d'Armes: the *Basilique Notre-Dame* (evening son et lumière show), the *Chapelle Notre-Dame-de-Bonsecours* and the *Château de Ramezay,* once the governor's residence, today a museum of the city's history. There is also the classical domed building of the *Marché Bonsecours* on the Rue St-Paul, where exhibitions often take place. And down on the river the piers of the *Vieux Port* lure visitors with an IMAX cinema, flea markets, boat trips and summer festivals. If you are tired of walking; why not allow yourself a massage or a spa treatment in the five-storey ● *Bota Bota Spa (www.botabota.ca)* on a refurbished old ferry?

FOOD & DRINK

INSIDER TIP CHEZ CORA (U C4) (*⬚ c4*)

A franchise of cosy snack bars, serving Montréal's most popular and cheapest breakfast with fruit, waffles and muesli.

1240, Rue Drummond (also 1017, Rue Ste-Catherine Est) | www.chezcora.com | Budget

CHEZ L'EPICIER (U E3) (*ᗰ e3*)
Modern, innovative Québecois cuisine in a historic building in the middle of the historic centre with an interior styled as a grocery store. 311, Rue St-Paul Est | tel. 514 8 78 22 32 | Expensive

LOW BUDGET

The *Montréal Museum Pass* will save you money at many of the museums: valid for three days the C$75 ticket will give you free admission to 41 (so almost all) city museums; for an extra C$5, the buses and subway are also free.

Eco-friendly ● ◑ *Bixi Bikes* are available in many locations throughout the city, they are a cheap transport alternative. The first half hour is included in the basic price. Payment by credit card: C$5/day, C$14/3 days. montreal.bixi.com

In the *Plateau* district or in the *Rue Prince-Arthur* and the *Rue Duluth*, many restaurants allow you to bring your own wine *(Apportez votre vin/ BYOW)*. The restaurant provides glasses and charges a small corkage fee.

In the heart of the old town is the clean, and also very cheap, *Auberge Alternative* (358, Rue St-Pierre | tel. 514 2 82 80 69 | www.auberge-alternative.qc.ca): a bed in the dormitory costs C$27 per night, a private room C$75 including tax.

L'EXPRESS (147 F3) (*ᗰ H12*)
A little piece of Paris where you can enjoy a perfect *steak frite* or *croque monsieur*. And the ambience of this restaurant in the 'in' district of Plateau is also spot on. 3927, Rue St-Denis | tel. 514 8 45 53 33 | Budget–Moderate

FIREGRILL (U B–C4) (*ᗰ b–c4*)
If you are a fan of meat dishes, this is the right place to go to, offering thick striploin steaks, juicy firegrill burgers and other celicacies, and situated in the vicinity of the nightlife district around the Rue Crescent in the west of the city. 1490, Rue Stanley | tel. 514 8 42 00 20 | Moderate–Expensive

LEMÉAC CAFÉ BISTRO (U A1) (*ᗰ a1*)
Classic French-Québecois cuisine in the Plateau Mont Royal district. If you wish, you can eat on the terrace. 1045, Ave. Laurier Ouest | tel. 514 2 70 09 99 | Moderate–Expensive

MAESTRO S.V.P. (U C2) (*ᗰ c2*)
For shellfish lovers: this bistro offers dozens of oyster and shellfish dishes, many originating in the Atlantic provinces of Canada. These are all on view in the huge display case at the entrance. 3615, Blvd. St-Laurent | tel. 514 8 42 64 47 | Moderate

RESTO VEGO ◑ (U D1–2) (*ᗰ d1–2*)
Small chain of vegetarian buffet restaurants with several branches in the city, e.g. in the centre of the student district, with pleasant terraces: 1720, Rue St-Denis | tel. 514 8 45 26 27 | Budget

SCHWARTZ' ★ (U B–C1) (*ᗰ b–c1*)
This classic Yiddish deli restaurant is famous for its smoked meat. For C$9 you can enjoy a hearty smoked meat sandwich, for C$17 a giant platter for the

Montréal's Ville Souterrain is considered the world's largest underground city

big appetite. *3895, Blvd. St-Laurent | tel. 514 8 42 48 13 | Budget*

XO LE RESTAURANT
Ideal for an elegant dinner or a sophisticated Sunday brunch: fine French-Canadian cuisine, served in the hall of an old bank. *355, Rue St-Jacques Ouest | tel. 514 8 41 50 00 | Expensive*

VILLE SOUTERRAINE ●
A weatherproof underground city that is a series of interconnected complexes that totals about 30 km/18.6 mi. Some 200 restaurants, 50 banks, 40 cinemas, theatres, concert halls and almost 2000 shops form part of the air-conditioned labyrinth in the belly of the city. *Entrance Rue Ste-Catherine*

SHOPPING

Department stores such as *The Bay* and numerous boutiques are situated on the *Rue Ste-Catherine.*

MARCHÉ JEAN-TALON ★
(147 F3) (⌀ H12)
The most attractive of Montréal's markets: from 8am there is lots of scrambling and jostling round the mountains of apples and artichokes. Excellent Québec products such as INSIDER TIP good jams and liqueurs can be found at *Le Marché des Saveurs. 7070 Ave. Henri-Julien*

TOURS

Apart from trips on the regular sightseeing buses, e.g. of *Grayline Tours (tel. 514 3 98 97 69)* there are also horse carriage trips. Points of departure on Dorchester Square. Boat tours through the harbour arranged by *Croisères AML (tel. 866 8 56 66 68)* and *Bateau Mouche (tel. 514 8 49 99 52).*

MONTRÉAL ON WHEELS (U E3) (⌀ e3)
Guided bicycle tours through the old town, along the St Lawrence and the Lachine Canal, also bicycle and rollerblade

rentals. *Daily 9am–8pm | tel. 877 8 66 06 33 | 27, Rue de la Commune Est | caroulemontreal.com*

ENTERTAINMENT

Experience ballet, theatre and opera in the *Place des Arts (telephonic ticket sales 514 8 42 2112)* performing arts centre. The city's nightlife concentrates at the mainly English speaking western end of the Rue Ste-Catherine and the Rue Crescent. People meet up here at *Winnie's (1455, Rue Crescent)*, in the *Sir Winston Churchill (1450, Rue Crescent)* or in the chic INSIDER TIP *Wienstein and Gavinos (1434, Rue Crescent)*. In the east the scene revolves around the Boulevard St-Laurent and the Rue St-Denis, some clubs are also in Vieux Montréal.

A popular meeting spot is the *Plage de l'Horloge* at the Clocktower Pier in the old town, Montréal's version of a trendy city beach. Especially popular among the young scene are the lounge clubs along the Boulevard St-Laurent, where you can chill out on sofas during the hot summer nights, for instance in the *Apt. 200 (3643, Blvd. St-Laurent)*, on the rooftop terrace of *Don B. Comber (3616 Blvd. St-Laurent)* or at *Blizzarts (3956 A, Blvd. St-Laurent)*.

The most popular venues are *Le Saint-Sulpice (1680, Rue St-Denis)*, *Madame Lee (151, Rue Ontario Est)* and the student meeting place *Café Campus (57, Rue Prince Arthur)*, where rock bands frequently perform. Good jazz at *Upstairs (1254, Rue MacKay | www. upstairsjazz.com)*.

WHERE TO STAY

ANNE MA SŒUR ANNE (U B1) (*ff b1*)
Cheerful yellow walls, narrow hallways, stairs and balconies transform this well-kept guesthouse into a labyrinth. But this is exactly what makes this old townhouse in the trendy Plateau Mont-Royal district so cosy and inviting. *17 rooms | 4119, Rue St-Denis | tel. 514 2 81 31 87 | www.anne masoeuranne.com | Budget–Moderate*

HOTEL 10 (U C2) (*ff c2*)
Trendy designer hotel only a few steps from the Place des Arts and Montréal's nightlife district, popular among actors and media people. Asian inspired restaurant and stylish bar. *136 rooms | 10, Rue Sherbrooke Ouest | tel. 514 8 43 60 00 | www.hotel10montreal. com | Expensive*

HOTEL GAULT (U E3) (*ff e3*)
A pilgrimage site for design fans. The historic Beaux Arts facade gives no indication of the avant-garde design inside: 1960s furniture (chairs by Pierre Paulin), futuristic lighting, polished wood floors and raw concrete walls. *30 rooms | 449, Rue Ste-Hélène | tel. 514 9 04 16 16 | www. hotelgault.com | Expensive*

HÔTEL DE PARIS (U D1) (*ff d1*)
Simple hotel in a historical house with winding stairways and rather small rooms. Although it has seen better days, the price and location are ideal. A youth hostel is adjoined. *39 rooms | 901, Rue Sherbrooke Est | tel. 514 5 22 68 61 | www. hotel-montreal.com | Budget–Moderate*

HÔTEL PLACE D'ARMES (U E3) (*ff e3*)
Elegant, small hotel in a stylishly renovated old building in the middle of Vieux Montréal. *133 rooms | 55, Rue St-Jacques Ouest | tel. 514 8 42 18 87 | www.hotel placedarmes.com | Moderate–Expensive*

LE ST-MARTIN ✪ (U C4) (*ff c4*)
Stylish, small city hotel, modern design. Right in the shopping area. *123 rooms |*

980, Blvd. Maisonneuve Ouest | tel. 514 8 43 30 00 | www.lestmartinmontreal. com | *Moderate–Expensive*

INFORMATION

INFOTOURISTE (U C4) (*ⓜ c4*)

Large information bureau and ticket office for concerts and sporting events. Provides information for all regions of Québec and reservations for overnight bookings and tours. *Daily in summer 9am–7pm, otherwise 9am–5pm | 1255, Rue Peel, Suite 100 | tel. 514 8 73 20 15, 877 2 66 56 87 (toll free) | www. mtl.org, www.quebecoriginal.com*

WHERE TO GO

CHAMBLY (148 A5) (*ⓜ H12*)

The small city (pop. 20,000), some 30 km/18.6 mi east of Montréal, is a good starting point for the Richelieu River valley tour, for centuries the most important connection from St Lawrence valley to the south. In the restored 1711 *Fort Chambly* the eventful history of this region – which was contested by the Iroquois, French, English and Americans – is evident.

LAURENTIDES ★ (147 F2) (*ⓜ H11*)

The mountain region of the Laurentides north of the city is about an hour's drive on Autoroute 15. This is the local recreational area for Montréalers. On weekends they come in droves to fish, hike, swim or ski. On weekdays you have the large forested area almost to yourself. You can find hotels and beautiful bathing lakes around *Sainte-Adèle* and *Sainte-Agathe-des-Monts.* In the *Parc du Mont-Tremblant* from 1894 you can go on hikes or bicycle tours and explore over 500 lakes and numerous waterfalls. In summer, rather luxurious accommodations in the ski village of Mont Tremblant are comparatively inexpensive. Well located in the pedestrian zone is *Ermitage du Lac (69 rooms | 150, Chemin du Curé-Deslauriers | tel. 514 6 81 22 22 | www.lessuitestremblant.com | Budget).*

Laurentides: Montréal's local recreational area

QUÉBEC

When you follow the St Lawrence east from the Great Lakes you will suddenly find yourself in another world: the road signs now say *Rue* or *Sortie* and no longer *Street* or *Exit*.

In the countryside there are old farming villages with French heritage farmhouses gathered around historic Catholic churches, while exuberant Montréal sparkles with Mediterranean esprit and the old town of Québec City, which celebrated its 410th anniversary in 2018, is a World Heritage Site that is surrounded by a historic city wall.

Québec, Canada's largest province is a linguistic and cultural bastion of France in British North America. The province was governed for many years by the *Parti Québecois* that pushed for independence. But since 2003 the Liberal Party has been in power and set back the separatist goals. Despite many American influences, the Gallic culture of Québec is still alive and kicking. It has even expanded its position in the last 40 years.

The St Lawrence River was the most important migration corridor in Canada. The French colonialists settled on the fertile, flat shore terraces on both sides of the mighty river 350 years ago. Today, about 90 per cent of the 8.4 million Québecers live in the region from Montréal to Québec City. Further eastwards, on the Gaspésie Peninsula and on the northern shore of river Saint Laurent, the settlements become more sparse and give way to

Photo: View of Pic de L'Aurore near Percé

A region of contrasts on the St Lawrence River: France's child in the New World is quaint and historic yet vibrant and modern

the scenic beauty of the *belle province*: the Parc national de Forillon, which is surrounded by 200 m/656 ft high cliffs, and the bizarre rock columns of the Mingan Archipelago are among the most impressive landscapes on the Atlantic.

The far north of the province, which encompasses almost four fifths of the land area of 580,000 mi², is almost uninhabited. It is a rocky landscape interspersed with lakes, and polished smooth by ice glaciers, that extends to Hudson Bay and to Ungava Bay on the Arctic Ocean.

The bedrock of the Canadian Shield in this region is the treasure chest of Québec with its large gold, copper and zinc deposits. The southern part of this rugged, unspoilt landscape, the densely wooded *Laurentian Mountains,* are easily accessible for tourists as they are full of parks for canoeing and rustic lodges that are ideal bases for extended hikes in the summer and for skiing in the snowy winter.

The flaming colour of the leaves transforms the landscape near Baie-St-Paul into a colourful spectacle

BAIE-COMEAU

(148 C2) (*M L9*) **The attractions of this small port city (pop. 23,000) on the secluded north shore of the St Lawrence lies deep in its forested hinterland: seven massive dams retain the Maniconagan and Outardes rivers and generate electricity.**

The dams *Manic 2* and the 150 m/492 ft *Manic 5* may be viewed by the public. A ferry connects Baie-Comeau with *Matane* on the southern shore of the St Lawrence thereby enabling a round trip along both shores of the river. Much closer along the eastern edge is the *Jardin des Glaciers (in summer daily 8am–5pm | admission C$24–33 | 3, Ave. Denonville)*, an adventure park with high-tech multimedia shows about the last Ice age and the actual global warming. ⚜ *Le Manoir*

(60 rooms | 8, Ave. Cabot | tel. 418 2 96 33 91 | www.manoirbc.com | Moderate) is an elegant old house with a view of the coast.

BAIE-ST-PAUL

(148 B3) (*M K10*) **The town (pop. 7300) in the hills on the northern shore of the St Lawrence has been drawing summer visitors and nature lovers for more than 100 years – and inspired artists.**

Here, the granite massif of the Canadian Shield meets the broad valley of the St Lawrence. Dramatic landscapes are guaranteed, especially during the autumn when its autumn foliage is the most beautiful in Canada. The old town buildings have numerous galleries, and sometimes the studios of contemporary and past painters of the region may also be visited, such as the *Maison René Richard (58, Rue St-Jean-Baptiste)*.

SIGHTSEEING

LE CARREFOUR CULTUREL PAUL-MÉDÉRIC
Exhibition space for paintings, installations and art events. *In summer Tue–Sun 10am–5pm | admission free | 4, Rue Ambroise-Fafard*

MUSÉE D'ART CONTEMPORAIN
Temporary exhibitions of diverse regional art, in a modern building. *In summer daily 10am–5pm | admission C$10 | 23, Rue Ambroise-Fafard*

TOURS

ÎLES AUX COUDRES
A car ferry runs from *St-Joseph-de-la-Rive* to the 16 km/9.9 mi long island with old mills and picturesque villages.

PARC NATIONAL DES GRANDS-JARDINS ★
This park, set in the bare hilltops of the Laurentides inland from Baie-St-Paul, is a Unesco biosphere reserve. Its expanse includes unusual subarctic vegetation, a remnant of the last ice age: meadows filled with white reindeer moss and a small forest of miniature pines reminiscent of the Taiga forest. Highly recommended: the four-hour ⚡ hiking trail to *Mont du Lac-des-Cygnes* with a magnificent panoramic view of the ancient meteorite crater, which formed the entire region *(access via Route 381 | info centre, exhibitions, hiking trails and camping)*. Immediately to the north where the Rivière Malbaie has carved out a INSIDER TIP spectacular, 500 m/1640 ft deep canyon in the granite of the Canadian Shield is the *Parc national des Hautes-Gorges-de-la-Rivière-Malbaie* with a pristine natural landscape, which you can also explore in a canoe. *Info for both parks tel. 418 4 39 12 27 | also canoe hire and camping*

WHERE TO STAY

AUBERGE AUX PETITS OISEAUX
Historic estate with various comfortably furnished houses and artist studios. This is where the founders of the *Cirque du Soleil* started their careers in the 1980s. *15 rooms | 30, Rue Ambroise-Fafard | tel. 418 7 60 82 88 | www.auxpetitsoiseaux.ca | Budget–Expensive*

LE GERMAIN CHARLEVOIX
Guy Laliberté, one of the founders of Cirque du Soleil, runs an innovative, ultra modern lodge with a nice Spa, lots

MARCO POLO HIGHLIGHTS

★ **Parc national des Grands-Jardins**
Through subarctic vegetation and deep gorges → p. 71

★ **Rocher Percé**
Spectacular sheer rock formation that rises up out of the ocean off the Gaspésie → p. 73

★ **Haute Ville & Basse Ville**
Québec's old town is the birthplace of Canada → p. 78

★ **Musée national de Beaux-Arts du Québec**
Fine art in an old prison → p. 78

★ **Île d'Orléans**
Idyllic villages and wide scenic views on the St Lawrence → p. 81

★ **Parc national de la Mauricie**
The ideal holiday destination for canoeists → p. 83

of art and a fine restaurant. *145 rooms | 50, Rue de la ferme | tel. 418 2 40 41 00 | www.legermainhotels.com* | Moderate–Expensive

AUBERGE DU RAVAGE 🌳

Ravage means moose pasture, and this wilderness lodge that is run according to ecological ideals (own small hydro-electric power plant) is true to its name. Good as a base for trips in the *Parc national des Hautes-Gorges. 12 rooms |*

156, Saint-Urbain | Pourvoire de Lac-Moreau, C.P. | tel. 418 6 65 44 00 | www.lacmoreau.com | with half or full board Moderate–Expensive

GASPÉSIE

(148–149 C–E 2–3) *(𝄞 L–M 9–10)* **The roughly 300 km/186 mi long peninsula extends out into the Gulf of St Lawrence and here you can experience some of most the impressive landscapes in Québec. A tour of the area is especially beautiful in autumn when the foliage becomes a riot of colour.**

SIGHTSEEING

GASPÉSIE ROUND TRIP

From Québec City the Route 132 takes you through picturesque farming villages on the south shore of the St Lawrence to *Montmagny* **(148 B4)** *(𝄞 K11).* Offshore, on the *Île aux Grues,* thousands of snow geese stop off in the late summer on their way south (boat tours). *St-Jean-Port-Joli* **(148 B3)** *(𝄞 K11)* is famous for its woodcarvers. The *Musée des Anciens Canadiens (May–Oct | admission C$8 | on Hwy 132)* highlights works by the Bourgault brothers.

Lighthouses, old villages and long beaches line the way to the east. From *Matane* **(149 D2)** *(𝄞 L9)* the coasts gets lonelier and rougher, the mountains closer to the widening river. The hinterland of the *Chic Choc Mountains,* which is characterised by subarctic vegetation, and which is one of the oldest mountain ranges in North America, is also home to the *Parc national de la Gaspésie (Route 299)* with moose, bears and caribou.

In the *Parc national du Canada Forillon* on the eastern tip of the Gaspésie Peninsula the mountains meet the sea: almost

200 m/656 ft ⚒ limestone cliffs tower over the crashing waves of the Atlantic. The southern coast of the park however, has numerous beaches and coves.

In *Gaspé* (149 E2) *(ⵡ N9)* (pop. 15,000), the main town on the peninsula, a monument on Hwy. 132 commemorates the discovery of the region by Jacques Cartier. Route 132 takes you south

summer daily 8.30am–6pm, July/Aug until 8pm | admission C$18 | Route 132 Grand-Métis, between Rimouski and Matane

PARC NATIONAL DE MIGUASHA (149 D3) *(ⵡ M10)*

It is almost beyond comprehension that the fossils in these cliffs are 380 mil-

An enormous limestone rock protrudes from the sea near the idyllic coastal village Percé

through the beautiful artist and fishing village *Percé*. The *Baie des Chaleurs* on the southern coast, which is surprisingly warm during the summer, is lovely and less rugged. Here you will find beautiful holiday resorts such as *Bonaventure* and *Carleton* with sandy beaches, hiking trails and salmon rivers.

JARDIN DE MÉTIS (148 C2) *(ⵡ L10)*

A wonderful garden that is transformed in the summer by designers from all over the world for an international garden festival. Today the old mansion houses art galleries and a museum dedicated to settler history. *During the*

lion years old. These include the most beautiful fossil fish in the world which explains why the park has been declared a Unesco World Heritage Site. *Open daily in summer 9am–5pm | admission C$18 | Nouvelle*

ROCHER PERCÉ ★ (149 E2) *(ⵡ N10)*

The massive, 90 m/295.3 ft reddish rock formation is the symbol of the peninsula and extends to the east near the village of *Percé* where it lies off the coast and protrudes from the breakers. At low tide you can walk on a sandbank and see fossils from the Devonian Period that are embedded in the shale rock.

TOURS

ESKAMER ADVENTURE

A few hours or the whole day: kayak trips along the St Lawrence coast. Also canoeing in the canyons of the hinterland. *292 Blvd. Perron Est | Ste-Anne-des-Monts | tel. 418 9 67 29 99 | www.eskamer.ca*

ÎLE BONAVENTURE

Boat trips to the bird cliffs of the island are offered. There is also a ferry service for hikers. Exhibitions in the *Centre de Découverte, Le Chafaud (4, Rue du Quay | Percé | tel. 418 7 82 22 40).*

LA SOCIÉTÉ DUVETNOR

Boat trips to the small islands in the lower St Lawrence region, bird watching, INSIDER TIP on request with overnight accommodation in a lighthouse or on a lonely island. *Rivière-du-Loup | tel. 418 8 67 16 60 | www.duvetnor.com*

WHERE TO STAY

AUBERGE FESTIVE SEA SHACK

Accommodation in 12 log cabins right on the coast, which offers also camping facilities. Hiking trails start right from the Auberge; tours to the Parc national de Forillon possible. *292, Blvd. Perron Est | Ste-Anne-des-Monts | tel. 418 7 63 29 99 | www.aubergefestive.com | Budget–Moderate*

CHÂTEAU LAMONTAGNE ☀

A pretty place and a nice house with a superb view of St Lawrence River. *7 rooms | 170, 1ere Ave. Est | Ste-Anne-des-Monts | tel. 418 7 63 76 66 | www.chateaulamontagne.com | Budget–Moderate*

CHIC-CHOCS MOUNTAIN LODGE

This comfortable wilderness lodge is located in a wildlife preserve high

Île Bonaventure is a paradise for birds – humans are tolerated only when fenced in

up in the mountains. *18 rooms | July–mid Sept | Route 132, approx. 55 km/34 mi south of Cap-Chat | tel. 800 6 65 30 91 | www.sepaq.com | Moderate–Expensive*

LA NORMANDIE ⚲

High up on the cliffs with a view of the Rocher Percé. Good restaurant. *45 rooms | 221, Route 132 Ouest | Percé | tel. 418 7 82 21 12 | www.normandieperce.com | Moderate*

INFORMATION

ASSOCIATION TOURISTIQUE RÉGIONALE DE LA GASPÉSIE
1020, Blvd. Jacques-Cartier | Mont-Joli | tel. 418 7 75 22 23 | www.tourisme-gaspesie.com

MAGOG

(148 A5) *(᎙ J12)* **The town (pop. 14,000) on the northern shore of the long Lac Memphrémagog lies in the heart of the Eastern Townships – and therefore in the centre of the holiday region with well-maintained hotels, golf courses, lakes and hiking trails in the forested foothills of the Appalachian Mountains that stretch across the nearby US border to Québec.**

From ⚲ *Mont Orford* you can get a view over the rolling countryside, taste the delicious cheese made by monks in the old Benedictine abbey *St-Benoît-du-Lac*, and admire the 1920s villas of the rich American summer visitors in *North Hatley.*

The town of *Coaticook* also deserves a detour to the *Parc de la Gorge de Coaticook* where a 170 m/558 ft high ⚲ pedestrian bridge leads you over a 750 m/2460 ft wide gorge.

MINGAN ARCHIPELAGO

(149 E–F1) *(᎙ N8)* **The route that Jacques Cartier followed from Québec City along the northern shore of the St Lawrence ends after about 650 km/404 mi in Havre Saint Pierre. It is situated on Pointeaux-Esquimaux. Here you can hire boat tours to the islands of the Parc national de l'Archipel Mingan.**

There the tidal ebb and flow has eroded the soft limestone into bizarre rock columns. On the more than 40 islands that lie off the coast in a long outstretched chain one can view numerous bird colonies and sometimes even whales in the very salty waters.

In *Longue-Pointe,* a large *Centre d'Interprétation (in summer daily 9am–5pm | admission C$10 | www.rorqual.com)* provides illustrated details about humpbacks, blue whales and fin whales. At certain times, you can go on an ● **INSIDER TIP** observation day trip with whale researchers from the *Mingan Island Cetacean Study (MICS) (cost C$140 | current information at www.rorqual.com/english/how-to-get-involved/day-trips)*. The park wardens and several boat companies offer half-day tours from Havre-Saint-Pierre to the most beautiful rock formations in the central part of the park *(ticket prices available from C$50 | www.parkscanada.ca)*.

QUÉBEC CITY

🔲 MAP ON P. 77
(148 B4) *(᎙ J11)* **The crooked and cobblestone alleys, stone city gates and fortified bastions of the medieval-looking old town of Québec City are unique in Canada.**

Upper and lower town of Québec City: French way of life and a host of historical buildings

The countless American tourists are enchanted by so much historic charm. The capital (pop. 810,000) of the province of Québec at the mouth of the St Charles into the St Lawrence has a long history – a rarity in the young Canada. In 2008 the city celebrated its 400-year anniversary since its establishment by Samuel de Champlain. Québec has been the French Canadian cultural and economic centre since the 17th century; in 1763 it fell into the hands of the British but it has continued to stay true to the French way of life.

For the most beautiful views of the city, you have to go on to the water: a ☀ *harbour cruise* is ideal for an exploration of the old harbour and the wide St Lawrence River. It is best to leave your car in the hotel car park during your visit to Québec. The compact old town is best explored on foot.

SIGHTSEEING

CATHÉDRALE NOTRE-DAME
(77 B2) (*Ø I2*)

The 1643 basilica (which was rebuilt after a fire in 1922) is the oldest parish church in North America. Many pioneers of New France are buried in the crypt. *In summer daily 7am–7pm, Sun from 8am (guided tours) | 16, Rue Buade*

LA CITADELLE (77 B4) (*Ø I4*)

The construction of this star-shaped fortress on the 110 m/361 ft *Cap aux Diamants* took 30 years to complete. The wide meadows in front of it were the scene for the decisive battle between the French and the English for the domination in America 1759. Guided tours and military museum, in the evening also lantern tours, creepiness included. *In summer daily 9am–5pm, changing of*

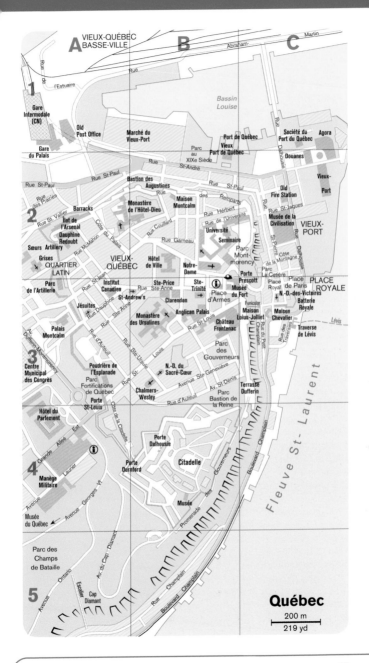

A VIEUX-QUÉBEC
BASSE-VILLE **B** Abraham- Martin **C**

1
Rue de l'Estuaire

Gare Intermodale (CN)

Old Post Office

Marché du Vieux-Port

Bassin Louise

Port de Québec

Vieux Port de Québec

Société du Port du Québec

Agora

Gare du Palais

Parc au XIXe Siècle

Douanes

Vieux-Port

Rue St-André

2
Rue St-Paul

Rue St-Paul

Rue des Prairies

Barracks

Îlot de l'Arsenal

Dauphine Redoubt

Sœurs Grises

Artillery

QUARTIER LATIN

Bastion des Augustines

Monastère de l'Hôtel-Dieu

Maison Montcalm

Côte du Palais

Rue Couillard

Rue Garneau

Rue St-Paul

des

Remparts

Rue Hébert

Rue de l'Université

Université

Séminaire

Old Fire Station

Rue St-Jaques

Musée de la Civilisation

VIEUX-PORT

Rue St-Pierre

VIEUX-QUÉBEC

Hôtel de Ville

Notre-Dame

Parc Montmorency

Porte Prescott

Côte de la Montagne

Parc La Cetière

PLACE ROYALE

Parc de l'Artillerie

Institut Canadien

St-Andrew's

Jésuites

Palais Montcalm

Ste-Price
Ste-Anne

Clarendon

Anglican Palais

Ste-Trinité

Place d'Armes

Musée du Fort

Place Royal

Place de Paris

N.-D.-des-Victoires

Batterie Royale

Maison Loius-Jolliet

Maison Chevalier

Lévis

3
Centre Municipal des Congrès

Monastère des Ursulines

Poudrière de l'Esplanade

Parc Fortifications de Québec

Porte St-Louis

N.-D. du Sacré-Coeur

Chalmers-Wesley

Château Frontenac

Parc des Gouverneurs

Avenue Ste-Geneviève

Av. St-Denis

Rue d'Auteuil

Parc Bastion de la Reine

Terrasse Dufferin

Fleuve St-Laurent

Hôtel du Parlement

Grande Allée Est

Laurier

Porte Dalhousie

Porte Ormford

Citadelle

4
Manège Militaire

Avenue Georges VI

Musée

Musée du Québec

5
Parc des Champs de Bataille

Ontario

Cap Diamant

Escalier

Av. du Cap-Diamant

Rue Champlain

Boulevard Champlain

Promenade des Gouverneurs

Québec

200 m
219 yd

QUÉBEC CITY

CITY **WHERE TO START?**
The **Terrasse Dufferin (77 B3)**
(*[map] I3*) outside the hotel **Le Château
Frontenac**. is the best place to get
a first overview. From here you can
walk or use the *funiculaire* to the
old town in the Rue de Petit Champlain, Place Royale and the Musée
de la Civilisation. Or you can stay in
Haute Ville and indulge in a shopping and dining spree on the Rue
St-Jean.
Parking: along the river next to the
ferry stop (50 Rue Dalhousie) or
in the upper town around Grande
Allée.

*the guard in summer daily 10am, mili-
tary tattoo in July/Aug Wed 5pm in the
citadel | admission C$16 | entrance from
the Rue St-Louis*

HAUTE VILLE & BASSE VILLE ★
(77 A–C 1–3) *([map] k–m 1–3)*

Basse Ville (the lower town) is located
on a narrow waterfront terrace on the St
Lawrence, where Samuel de Champlain
first built a small fortress. In the Rue de
Petit-Champlain and around the Place
Royal with the church *Notre-Dame-des-
Victoires* (1688) are old buildings filled
with galleries, cafés and souvenir shops.
This district of the old town has been
designated by Unesco as a Cultural World
Heritage Site. Signs provide information
on the location of the first fur trading
fort and other buildings errected by
Champlain. Inside these buildings, many
ancient walls and vaults have survived.
Haute Ville (the higher part) is further
up on a steep hill and is dominated by
the splendid hotel *Le Château Frontenac*,
which was completed in 1924. Presidents
and kings have slept under its copper roof.

All around it the narrow alleys of the old
town are squeezed in side by side, surrounded by the city wall: the lively *Place
d'Armes,* the [icon] viewing promenade the
Terrasse Dufferin and the *Rue St-Louis* with
its many 17th century houses.

MUSÉE DE LA CIVILISATION
(77 C2) *([map] m2)*
Temporary exhibitions about the cultural
history of Québec in a spectacular mu-
seum building. *Tue–Sun 10am–5pm | ad-
mission C$16 | 85, Rue Dalhousie | www.
mcq.org*

MUSÉE NATIONAL DES BEAUX-ARTS
DU QUÉBEC ★ **(148 B4)** *([map] J11)*
A comprehensive chronology of art in
the province: paintings, sculptures and
typical craftwork. Also a new, excellent
Inuit art exhibition and a sculpture by Da-
vid Moore in the old prison tower. *Daily
10am–6pm, Wed until 9pm, winter until
5pm and closed on Mon | admission C$20 |
179, Grande Allée Ouest | www.mnba.org*

PARC DE L'ARTILLERIE **(77 A3)** *([map] k3)*
Exhibition about the city fortifications.
Large model of Québec from 1808. *Daily
10am–5pm, closed Oct–March | admissi-
on C$4 | 2, Rue d'Auteuil*

FOOD & DRINK

Even the smaller restaurants serve excellent quality meals. Ask for the mostly inexpensive *tables d'hôte* (daily specials).
The restaurants often require you to
make lunch reservations.

INSIDER TIP LE CASSE-CRÊPE BRETON
(77 A2) *([map] k2)*
Affordable and good: generously filled
crêpes in an often full, small restaurant.
*1136, Rue St-Jean | tel. 418 6 92 04 38 |
Budget–Moderate*

COSMOS CAFÉ (77 A4) *(🗺 k4)*
Popular, pleasant *brasserie* with excellent breakfast. *575, Grande Allée Est | tel. 418 6 40 06 06 |* Budget–Moderate

LE LAPIN SAUTÉ (77 C3) *(🗺 m3)*
French country cuisine at reasonable prices in the Basse Ville. With terrace. *52, Rue Petit Champlain | tel. 418 6 92 53 25 |* Moderate

CHEZ RIOUX ET PETTIGREW (77 C2) *(🗺 m2)*
Modern cuisine served within old masonry; traditional regional products such as venison and mushrooms are also on the menu. *48, Rue St-Paul | tel. 418 6 94 44 48 |* Budget–Moderate

INSIDER TIP NOCTUM (149 B4) *(🗺 J11)*
Cool decor, inspired Quebec cuisine and in-house-brewed designer beers: this is how a restaurant should be in the chic fashionable district St Roch on the northern edge of the old town.

438, rue du Parvis | tel. 581 7 42 79 79 | Moderate

INSIDER TIP SAGAMITÉ ☯ (148 B4) *(🗺 J11)*
Very good Native American organic restaurant in the hills along the city's edge. Many wild game dishes and regional products. Also a Native American museum and a very appealing hotel with a natural wood interior. The journey there is worthwhile. *10, Blvd. Maurice-Bastien | Wendake | tel. 418 8 47 69 99 |* Moderate

SHOPPING

MARCHÉ DU VIEUX-PORT ☯ (77 A–B1) *(🗺 k–l1)*
Products from Québec are fresh and cheap here: cranberry jelly, honey, cider, chocolates, *tarte au sucre*. Many also organic. *Daily 9am–6pm, Sat/Sun until 5pm, winter only Thu–Sun | 160, Quai St-André | www.marchevieuxport.com*

Rue de Petit Champlain – one of the many charming streets of Basse Ville

ENTERTAINMENT

The most popular street for an evening stroll is the *Grande Allée* outside the city wall. During the summer the cafés put tables outside on the pavements; *chansonniers* strum their guitars and the younger crowd meets up in the bars and cafés. Favourite venues here include *Chez Dagobert (600, Grande Allée)* and *Chez Maurice (575, Grande Allée)*. A massive variety of beer awaits you in the old town in the *Pub Saint-Alexandre (1087, Rue St-Jean)*.

WHERE TO STAY

LE 253 (148 B4) (*M J11*)
Bright, colourful and clean B&B styled with loving care in the young trendy district St. Roch. The city centre is only a 15-20-minute walk away. *3 rooms | 253, Rue de la Reine | tel. 418 6 47 05 90 | www. le253.com | Budget*

LE CHÂTEAU FRONTENAC
(77 B3) (*M I3*)
The landmark of the city: a palatial traditional hotel in the centre of the old town with an impressive guest list. ♫ Piano bar with beautiful view. Fitness centre and spa. *611 rooms | 1, Rue des Carrières | tel. 418 6 92 38 61 | www.fairmont.com/ frontenac-quebec | Expensive*

CLARENDON
(77 B2–3) (*M I2–3*)
This historic hotel dating from 1870 is plush and comfortable. Modestly modernised it is ideally situated at the heart of the old town. Diana Krall is one of the artists who have sung in the house jazz bar. *143 rooms | 57 Rue Sainte-Anne | tel. 418 6 92 24 80 | www.hotelclarendon. com | Moderate*

HÔTEL LE PRIORI
(77 C2) (*M m2*)
Postmodern meets the colonial era: designer hotel in a 1766 priory that is very peaceful, in the old town. *26 rooms | 15, Rue Sault-au-Matelot | tel. 418 6 92 39 92 | www.hotellepriori.com | Moderate–Expensive*

HÔTEL LE SAINT-PAUL
(77 B2) (*M I2*)
Pleasant mid-range hotel in a historic building close to the harbour, with restaurant. *27 rooms | 229, Rue St-Paul | tel. 418 6 94 44 14 | www.lesaintpaul.qc.ca | Moderate*

INFORMATION

OFFICE DU TOURISME DE QUÉBEC
(77 B2–3) (*M I2–3*)
12, Rue Ste-Anne | tel. 418 6 41 62 90 | www.quebecregion.com

POUTINE – HOT & GREASY

In English speaking Canada there are hamburgers, hot dogs and potato chips on every corner. The Québecers on the other hand are proud of their culinary tradition and haute cuisine, influenced by the Gallic motherland.

Yet their secret national dish is *poutine*: a mix of potato chips topped with cheese curds and doused in gravy. In no time the crispy, crunchy chips become a peculiar greasy mush. Bon appétit!

WHERE TO GO

CÔTE DE BEAUPRÉ (148 B3–4) (*∅ J–K11*)

Great for a day trip: Avenue Royale, the 'road of the kings', Route 360 to the northern shore of the St Lawrence, which is steeped in history. The *Bellanger-Girardin House* in Beauport, which was built in 1673 in the Norman style, deserves a stop as does the 83 m/272.3 ft *Montmorency* waterfalls. Above the falls

Canyon Ste-Anne; at the *Cap Tourmente* 300,000 snow geese start their journey to the south in September. Above the river in the Canyon *Ste-Anne* is an adventure playground for the brave with fixed rope routes, rope bridges and several ziplines around a ravine including a 70 m/229.7 ft high waterfall *(daily 9am–6pm | admission C$13.50 | 206, Route 138 Est | Beaupré | tel. 418 8 27 40 57 | www. canyonsa.qc.ca).*

Canada's most famous pilgrim destination: Scala Santa of the Basilica of Ste-Anne-de-Beaupré

is the ☼ *Manoir Montmorency (tel. 418 6 63 33 30 | Moderate)*, a restaurant serving Québecois cuisine that also has a beautiful view. And the history of the region is documented in a visitor centre housed in a 1695 mill in *Château-Richer (7007, Ave. Royale).*

North America's most famous pilgrimage site is *Ste-Anne-de-Beaupré.* In the basement of the Saint Anne basilica – the patron saint of sailors – which was completed in 1923, numerous discarded crutches are evidence of the wonders of the pilgrimage site. Located nearby is a suspension bridge that spans deep

ÎLE D'ORLÉANS ★
(148 B4) (*∅ K11*)

Farming villages with picturesque churches are set against the peaceful backdrop of the wide river – as if time has stood still on this 30 km/18 mi long island. On a ☼ circular road you can enjoy views of Québec City and the St Lawrence and taste some of the farmers' products at road stalls: maple syrup, honey, cider, strawberries. Great stops: the small *Manoir Mauvide-Genest* museum in Saint-Jean and lunch at *Ancien Moulin (tel. 418 8 29 38 88 | Moderate)* of 1720 in Saint-Laurent.

SAGUENAY REGION

(148 B–C 2–3) (*① J–K10*) **The Sague-nay River flows from Lac Saint-Jean to St Lawrence in a fjord valley cut deep by glaciers.**

In summer, beluga and blue whales gather during near the river mouth at *Tadoussac* and can often be seen on ferry trips across the bay or special whale watching tours *(Saguenay day cruise organised by Croisières du Fjord | Chicoutimi | tel. 418 5 43 76 30 | www.croisieres aml.com)*.

In the 116 mi² *Parc du Saguenay,* steep cliffs tower up 400 m/1312 ft high around the ☆ *Baie Éternité.* You will find wonderful hiking trails with fantastic vantage points. At the upper end of the fjord lies the commercial port of *Chicoutimi,* one of the early industrial towns in Québec.

The origin of the Saguenay, *Lac Saint-Jean,* is an almost perfectly round lake from the last ice age with a surface of 500 mi². It is a popular sailing area and holiday destination with beautiful beaches.

SIGHTSEEING

CIMM (148 C3) (*① K10*)
Large exhibition centre of a whale research organisation; film screenings and `INSIDER TIP` boat trips to the belugas at Saguenay. *In summer daily 9am–8pm | admission C$12 | at Tadoussac harbour | baleinesendirect.org/gremm*

LA PULPERIE (148 B2) (*① K10*)
Fascinating industrial museum in a 100-year old wood pulp factory. Also theatre performances. *In summer daily 9am–6pm | admission C$14.50 | 300, Rue Dubuc | Chicoutimi | www.pulperie.com*

VAL JALBERT (148 A2) (*① J10*)
The former industrial village on the shore of Lac Saint-Jean is an open-air museum. Behind the sawmill is a 72 m/236.2 ft waterfall. Restaurant, cabins and rooms to rent. *In summer daily 9am–6pm | admission C$84 | www.valjalbert.com*

FOOD & DRINK

CHEZ MARIO TREMBLAY
(148 B2) (*① J10*)
Restaurant owned by a legendary hockey player. Burgers, salads, steaks. *Rue Collard Ouest | Alma | tel. 418 6 68 72 31 | Budget*

LA VOIE MALTÉE (148 B2) (*① K10*)
Brewery and pub with innovative beer dishes, terrace, often music on weekends. *777, Blvd Talbot | Chicoutimi | tel. 418 5 49 41 41 | Budget–Moderate*

WHERE TO STAY

TADOUSSAC (148 C3) (*① K10*)
Historic hotel, nostalgic summer resort on St Lawrence. *149 rooms | Tadoussac |*

tel. 418 2 35 44 21 | www.hoteltadoussac.com | Moderate–Expensive

INFORMATION

ASSOCIATION TOURISTIQUE RÉGIO-NALE DU SAGUENAY-LAC-ST-JEAN
(148 B2) (*🗺 K10*)
412, Blvd. Saguenay Est, Bureau 100 | Chicoutimi | tel. 418 5 43 97 78 | www.saguenaylacsaintjean.ca

TROIS-RIVIÈRES

(148 A4) (*🗺 J11*) **The old industrial city (pop. 160,000) on the banks of the St Lawrence, west of Québec City, is primarily a good starting point for trips into the St-Maurice Valley.**
On the St-Maurice River large quantities of wood are still floated downriver from the hinterland. And in the old town (the *vielle-ville*) of the fur trading post, which was established in 1634, you will still find many houses

from the 18th century around the picturesque town hall square and the Rue des Ursulines.

SIGHTSEEING

FORGES DU SAINT-MAURICE
Canada's first industrial village! The informative industrial museum shows the oldest ironworks in Canada, dating back to 1730. *In summer daily 10am–5pm | admission C$4 | 10000, Blvd. des Forges)*

WHERE TO GO

PARC NATIONAL DE LA MAURICIE ★
(148 A4) (*🗺 H–J11*)
The national park with many lakes and forests about 40 km/24.9 mi north-west of the city protects the typical landscape of the Canadian Shield and is a good bet for canoeists wanting to make day (or longer) trips *(rental at the info centres at the park entrances)*. The St-Maurice Valley on the eastern edge of the park – a holiday region with hotels and golf courses – is also suitable for hiking.

Glaciers from the last ice age created many lakes in Parc national de la Mauricie

ATLANTIC COAST

Silent mudflats and dramatic fjord coasts, deep forests and untamed rivers – the Atlantic region is in many ways reminiscent of the beautiful landscapes of Scotland or Norway.

The three Atlantic provinces (for the geographic and culturally distinct province Newfoundland & Labrador see p. 98), where Scots, Englishmen and Frenchmen have settled centuries ago, are a surprisingly diverse holiday destination.

The province of Nova Scotia offers old harbour towns, but also nice vineyards and the famous Cabot Trail that stretches above the cliffs of Cape Breton Island. The tiny island province of Prince Edward Island that is connected to the mainland by a gigantic bridge gives a completely different impression than Nova Scotia: it shows a pastoral landscape with picture-perfect villages and long, white sandy beaches. New Brunswick, the heavily forested province, is famous for the highest tidal fluctuation in the world. The seabed dries up for miles during low tide – that makes it ideal for a walk. And the sea provides food too. Restaurants in the harbour villages of New Brunswick serve freshly caught lobster, Atlantic salmon and exquisite oysters at moderate prices. The best place to start a round trip through the region (season is from the end of May–beginning of October) is in Halifax, which has an international airport and an extensive tourist infrastructure. Only few people – mostly fishermen and peasants – live off the bigger towns.

Barren land, rich sea: the wild north Atlantic characterises the life in the provinces of the east

ANNAPOLIS ROYAL

(149 E5) *(Ⓜ M12)* **Surrounded by orchards and picturesque farmlands, this small village (pop. 500) lies close to Digby on the Bay of Fundy in the north-west of Nova Scotia.**

Victorian houses line the streets of the little town with its old British Fort Anne and historic gardens. The town's history goes back a long way: Samuel de Champlain founded the *Habitation Port Royal (in summer 9am–5.30pm | admission C$4)* the first settlement in Canada, on the opposite bank of the *Annapolis Valley* in 1605. There are re-enactments at the fort where costumed guides demonstrate the pioneer life in 1605. The *tidal power plant* on the town's outskirts makes use of the Bay of Fundy's high tides. Good exhibitions in the plant's *Interpretive Centre (236 Prince Albert Rd.)*.

Travel back into the year 1744: Forteresse de Louisbourg

Do not forget to try the *Digby scallops*, which are brought in by the fishing fleet of the port of Digby and delivered to the restaurants. *Garrison House Inn (7 rooms | 350 St George St. | tel. 902 5 32 57 50 | www.garrisonhouse.ca | Budget–Moderate)* is a historic hotel with restaurant.

CAPE BRETON ISLAND

(150 B5) (*ⱷ O–P11)* **'Ciad mile failte!' A hundred thousand welcomes! The old Gaelic greeting is still often heard on Cape Breton Island.**

For more than 200 years the Scots have settled on this 4000 mi² island in the east of Nova Scotia. It is understandable that they should feel so at home here because the barren highlands and rugged coasts are amazingly similar to the Scottish Highlands.

SIGHTSEEING

ALEXANDER GRAHAM BELL NATIONAL HISTORIC SITE

Large museum next to Bell's home. Bell invented the telephone and did pioneering research on the hydrofoil and on aeronautics. *In summer 9am–5pm | admission C$8 | Baddeck*

CAPE BRETON ISLAND SIGHTSEEING TRIP

An island sightseeing trip is full of history and spectacular nature. Start at the beautifully situated resort of *Baddeck* in the north of the 70 km/43.5 mi long saltwater *Bras d'Or Lake* in the island interior. On a day trip you can go from Baddeck around the 300 km/186 mi long ★ ● ⟳ *Cabot Trail* of the northern tip of the island. It is famous for being the most beautiful scenic road in Eastern Canada: isolated cliffs and quiet tracts of moors, red granite rocks that glisten in the spray and tiny fishing villages with stacks of wooden lobster traps. Has all this given you an appetite? If so, you must try INSIDER TIP ▶ *Oceanside Chowder*. The three sisters in the small shack right at the end of the street in *Meat Cove* are fantastic cooks.

The prettiest part of the route runs through the *Cape Breton Highlands National Park* (great hiking trails). Near the northern entrance of the park you will suddenly hear new sounds – French. The small *Chéticamp* is an enclave of the Acadians. Their ancestors, French settlers from Nova Scotia and New Brunswick, fled from the English in 1755 to this inhospitable region. In the *Acadian Museum* and in the various galleries you can admire their traditional craftwork.

Take Hwy. 22 on a detour to the south of the island, past coalfields and the port town *Sydney*, from where the ferry leaves for Newfoundland.

FORTERESSE DE LOUISBOURG ★

Soldiers on parade, haggling fur traders and governing aristocrats – this living museum is an exact replica of life in 1744. The history depicted here is quite unaltered, to such an extent that both restaurants in the museum town use recipes from the 18th century. *In summer daily 9.30am–5pm | admission C$18 | Louisbourg*

FOOD & DRINK

CHANTERELLE ☺

Organically grown produce is used in this restaurant serving excellent regional cuisine. In the summer you will often see fresh *chanterelles* from the forest on the menu. The restaurant is part of the comfortable solar-powered *Chanterelle Country Inn* with 12 rooms and cabins. *48678 Cabot Trail | Baddeck | tel. 866 2 77 05 77 |*

www.chanterelleinn.com | Moderate–Expensive

KELTIC LODGE ☽

Elegant hotel restaurant serving regional specialities such as lobster and Solomon Gundy, and it also has a breath-taking view. *Ingonish Beach | tel. 902 2 85 28 80 | www.kelticlodge.ca | Moderate*

RED SHOE PUB

Enjoy the local character: fiddle music has always played a major role in the popular pub run by the musician family Rankin, augmented by good wholesome regional cooking. There is live music almost every evening: you can find the programme at *www.redshoepub.com. 11573 Hwy. 19 | Mabou | tel. 902 9 45 29 96 | Budget–Moderate*

SPORT & ACTIVITIES

KAYAK CAPE BRETON

Would you be interested in guided kayaking tours on the Bras d' Or Lake and along the coast? In addition to canoe, kayak and bicycle rental, there are also three log cabins available. *West Bay | tel. 902 5 35 30 60 | www.kayakcapebreton.com*

WHALE WATCHING

Along the northern coast of the island there are boat trips to the bird islands and sea caves in the summer, e.g. in *Pleasant Bay* by *Captain Mark's (tel. 902 2 24 13 16 | www.whaleandsealcruise.com)*. Many boat tours offer a money-back guarantee if you do not see any whales, or you can go on the trip again the next day.

WHERE TO STAY

DUNCREIGAN COUNTRY INN

This modern B&B is situated in an idyllic location nestling among trees on the Mabou River. *8 rooms | 11409 Hwy. 19 | Mabou | tel. 902 9 45 22 07 | www.duncreigan.ca | Moderate*

INVERARY INN ☆

Well maintained hotel with a view over the Bras d'Or Lake. Excellent cuisine.

138 rooms | Baddeck | tel. 902 2 95 35 00 | inveraryinn.com | Moderate–Expensive

INSIDER TIP VOLLMERS ISLAND PARADISE

Small log cabin lodge, on the south coast of Cape Breton with own diving base. *8 rooms | West Arichat | tel. 902 2 26 15 07 | www.vipilodge.com | Budget–Moderate*

INFORMATION

TOURISM CAPE BRETON

Info centre in Port Hastings and Sydney | tel. 902 5 63 46 36 | www.cbisland.com

CARAQUET

(149 E3) (∅ M10) The harbour town (pop. 4100) on the Baie des Chaleurs in the north-east of New Brunswick is the centre of the Péninsule Acadienne, an Acadian settler district.

Here, both the language and the old French culinary arts are still maintained. The *Village Historique Acadien (June–early Sept daily 10am–6pm | admission C$20 | Hwy. 11, approx. 10 km/6.2 mi west of Caraquet | www.villagehistoriqueacadien.com)* is an extensive museum village that represents the pioneer life and

ALEXANDER GRAHAM BELL

The United States have Thomas Edison and Canada has Alexander G. Bell (1847–1922). The Scottish-born Bell found fame in Ontario with his invention of the telephone in 1875. His Bell Telephone Company continues his legacy today in the form of the telecoms giant AT&T. Bell began his experiments in Nova Scotia in 1886 in the fields of medicine, aviation and marine technology and also developed the iron lung and special education methods for the deaf – a personal concern, because both his mother and his wife were deaf.

History of survival: in Kings Landing things are as they were in the mid 19th century

handicraft skills of the French settlers. 'Acadians' in costume plough the fields, work in the blacksmith's shop and serve in the tavern. You can enjoy Acadian cuisine in a house dating back to 1891 in the *Hotel Paulin (143, Blvd. St-Pierre Ouest | tel. 506 7 27 99 81 | Moderate)*

FREDERICTON

(149 D4) (*M11–12*) In the valley of the Saint John River, the capital of New Brunswick (pop. 60,000) has a small town atmosphere with its well-kept gardens and attractive buildings.

Originally founded by the French, many British loyalists moved here from the United States in 1785. The military buildings on Queen Street (which are used as museums), the English neo-Gothic *Christ Church Cathedral* in the city centre and the beautifully situated *University of New Brunswick* all attest to the influence of the British. The *Historic Garrison District*, which is good for a stroll and a browse, attracts with concerts, street theatre and films in the summer evenings.

SIGHTSEEING

BEAVERBROOK ART GALLERY
Excellent art museum with paintings by William Turner and Thomas Gainsborough. *Tue–Sun 10am–5pm, Thu until 9pm, Sun from noon, winter closed on Mon | admission C$10 | 703 Queen St. | www.beaverbrookartgallery.org*

KINGS LANDING
When a dam was built on the Saint John River, 25 historical buildings were saved from flooding and used to recreate a British loyalist village from the 18th century. Theatrical 'citizens' serve hearty food in the *King's Head Inn. Early June–early Oct daily 10am–5pm | admission C$18 on Hwy. 2 | 35 km/21.8 mi west of Fredericton*

SHOPPING

Saturday mornings are a social affair at the INSIDER TIP farmers' market on George Street. Regional farmers offer organic vegetables and regional specialities such as Fiddlehead fern tips and blueberries.

INFORMATION

TOURISM NEW BRUNSWICK
Visitor centre at the town hall | Queen St. | tel. 800 5 61 01 23 | www.tourism newbrunswick.ca

FUNDY NAT. PARK

(149 E5) (*M12*) **The hilly hinterland of the almost 80 mi² park on the south coast of New Brunswick ends at the shore of the Bay of Fundy with its almost 60 m/196.9 ft high cliffs.**
The funnel shaped bay has an especially impressive tidal range – the largest fluctuation in the world. During the high tide the water is at 10 m/32.8 ft while during low tide you can walk around on the dry mud flats *(guided tours by park wardens)*. Or you can hike on your own on the INSIDER TIP *Coastal Trail* from *Herring Cove* along the forested coast to *Matthews Head* (4.5 km/2.8 mi).

Some 40 km/24.9 mi east of the park at *Hopewell Cape*, the tidal range is particularly evident: during high tide the ★ *Flower Pot Rocks* are small islands, six hours later these rocks tower up 15 m/49.2 ft from the dried up seabed. The INSIDER TIP restaurant in the *Cape D'Or Lighthouse (Advocate Harbour | tel. 1 902 6 70 83 14 | www.capedor.ca | Budget–Moderate)* serves fabulous fish with a grand view. *Captains Inn B & B* is a cosy B & B in an old villa close to the parking entrance *(8 rooms | Alma | tel. 506 8 87 20 17 | www.captainsinn.ca | Budget)*.

HALIFAX

(149 F5) (*N12*) **The capital of Nova Scotia (pop. 425,000) is not only the economic and cultural centre of this province, but also of the whole Canadian Atlantic region.**

Tidal erosion: the Flower Pot Rocks are visible at low tide only

Halifax is a hard working port city with an over 25 km/15.5 mi long natural harbour. But on Friday and Saturday the city has – quite unusual in Canada – an active nightlife in the city centre. There are also the students from five universities that help to give the city its youthful image.

At the same time, Halifax is very proud of its age and historic sights. In the year 1749 the English chose the ice-free, strategically situated bay as a base and established a fort on the steep hill overlooking the harbour. Under the protection of the citadel, which emerged from this fort, Halifax blossomed into a rich trading town. No shot has ever been fired from the fortress, but ship convoys left from here for England during WW I & II.

> **CITY WHERE TO START?**
> The waterfront – naturally. From there, take a stroll through the **Historic Properties** and stop in at the Maritime Museum with its 'Titanic' exhibition. From here it is only a short distance uphill to George Street and the Grand Parade park and then another short stretch to the Town Clock at the Halifax Citadel.
> Parking: directly at the foot of George Street and next to the Maritime Museum, not only for cars but also for mobile homes. Several buses stop at Water Street.

SIGHTSEEING

HALIFAX CITADEL ☆
The fortress was built between 1828 and 1856 and has a commanding position overlooking the city centre. Today the building houses a military museum and its four-sided *Town Clock* is a Halifax landmark. *In summer 9am–6pm, otherwise until 5pm | admission C\$12, in low season C\$8*

HARBOURFRONT
The warehouses and piers along the Lower Water Street once belonged to the king's pirates who stowed their booty here. Today, boutiques and bars are lined along the attractively restored waterfront district. Especially successful is the *Historic Properties* complex with its narrow alleys and 19th century warehouses.

CITY CENTRE
The historic centre of the city is the *Grand Parade*, a small park flanked by the *town hall* and *St Paul's Church*, the oldest Anglican Church in Canada, which was built in 1750.

Further down the slope lies *Province House* (1818), the parliamentary seat of Nova Scotia, built in an elegant Georgian style.

MARITIME MUSEUM ●
Discover some interesting facts about sailing and steam shipping in the North Atlantic. And you can also view numerous INSIDER TIP items from the 'Titanic'. *Daily 9.30am–5.30pm, Tue until 8pm, otherwise Tue–Sat 9.30am–5pm, Sun 1pm–5pm | admission C\$9.55 | 1675 Lower Water St. | maritimemuseum. novascotia.ca*

PIER 21 – CANADA'S IMMIGRATION MUSEUM
Fascinating museum telling the story of immigration from Europe between 1928 and 1971. *In summer daily 9.30am–5.30pm, otherwise Tue–Sat 10am–5pm | admission C\$13 | 1055 Marginal Rd. | www.pier21.ca*

Famous historical sailing ships are often moored in the harbour of the Maritime Museum

FOOD & DRINK

MCKELVIE'S
Popular seafood restaurant, housed in an old fire station. *1680 Lower Water St. | tel. 902 4 21 61 61 | Moderate*

SALTY'S ON THE WATERFRONT ☆
Good choice for salmon and lobster: the upper floor offers fine dining, while on the ground floor you can enjoy breakfast and lunch. *Historic Properties | 1877 Upper Water St. | tel. 902 4 23 68 18 | Moderate–Expensive*

INSIDER TIP ▶ SPLIT CROW ●
Rustic bar in the old town, in the evenings they often have live music. To see who is playing visit *www.splitcrow.com. 1855 Granville St. | tel. 902 4 22 43 66 | Budget*

THE WOODEN MONKEY ☯
Only regional, macrobiotic products are used in the dishes of this popular restaurant in the old town. Delicious blueberry and apple turnover with maple syrup. *1707 Grafton St. | tel. 902 4 44 38 44 | Budget–Moderate*

SHOPPING

Galleries, souvenirs, Native American crafts and nautical bric-à-brac can be found in the *Historic Properties*. Shopping malls and various boutiques are situated on *Duke Street* and along *Spring Garden Road*. Find arts and crafts made in Nova Scotia in the *Centre for Craft and Design (1061 and 1096 Marginal Road)*. There is also a daily *farmers' market (Marginal Rd)* in the harbour with jams, smoked fish and many other regional products and artworks.

TOURS

COASTAL ADVENTURES
Kayak tours (one or several days) along the east coast of Nova Scotia. Also kayak rentals. *Tangier | tel. 902 7 72 27 74 | www.coastaladventures.com*

MURPHY'S – THE CABLE WHARF

Harbour sightseeing trips on the 'Harbour Queen' paddle steamer, the tall ship 'Shiva' or on the amphibious 'Harbour Hopper'. *Prices C$30–75 | Cable Wharf | tel. 902 4 20 10 15 | www.mtcw.ca*

ENTERTAINMENT

The nightlife of Halifax is concentrated in the bars and clubs around the *Grand Parade* and in the *Historic Properties,* such as the *Lower Deck* and *The Dome (1726 Argyle St.),* which is a complex with multiple dance floors.

WHERE TO STAY

LORD NELSON

Renovated old hotel opposite the beautiful Halifax Public Gardens. *260 rooms | 1515 South Park St. | tel. 902 4 23 63 31 | www.lordnelsonhotel.ca | Moderate–Expensive*

WAVERLEY INN

A charming inn on the southern edge of the old town. *34 rooms | 1266 Barrington St. | tel. 902 4 23 93 46, 800 5 65 93 46 | www.waverleyinn.com | Moderate*

INFORMATION

DEPARTMENT OF TOURISM

Bureau in front of the Maritime Museum | 1655 Lower Water St. | tel. 902 4 25 57 81, 800 5 65 05 11 | www.novascotia.com

WHERE TO GO

PEGGY'S COVE ★ ●
(149 F5–6) (*ɷ N12*)

A lighthouse perched on wave-swept granite rocks with colourful fishing cottages. This is Peggy's Cove (only 60 residents, approx. 45 km/28 mi south-west of Halifax) and it is considered to be the most picturesque fishing harbour on the Atlantic. It gets very busy in summer – but nevertheless the trip there is still worthwhile.

Just south of the village, a simple but moving monument commemorates the victims of the Swissair plane crash of September 1998.

KOUCHI-BOUGUAC NAT. PARK

(149 E4) (*ɷ M–N11*) **Salt marshes, sand dunes, lagoons and wonderful sandy beaches are the attractions of this 92 mi² sanctuary near Chatham.**

LOW BUDGET

For just C$7 you can taste North America's only single malt whiskey on Cape Breton Island in the *Glenora Distillery (in summer daily 9am–5pm | Route 19 | Glenville)* – including guided tour.

Many Indian, Vietnamese and Thai restaurants like *Baan Thai (5234 Blowers St. | Halifax | tel. 902 4 46 43 01)* offer lunch menus for only C$12.

Throughout the summer in Halifax there are free Sunday concerts in the ● *Public Gardens (Spring Garden Rd./South Park St.).* Fiddle music, country, rock – always a mixture – and a feast for the eyes because the garden is one of Canada's oldest.

The park has almost 50 km/31.1 mi of cycle paths leading through the dunes (bicycles available at *Ryan's Rental Centre* close to the campsite). Half-day tours in large *voyageur* canoes set out from *Cape St Louis (tel. 506 8 76 24 43)*.

LUNENBURG

(149 E6) (∅ N13) Many of the almost 3000 residents of this pretty fishing harbour on the south coast of Nova Scotia are descendants of the Germans and Swiss who settled here around 1750.

The 'Bluenose' schooner – which won many sailing regattas and adorns the 10 cent coin – was built here in 1921. The village is characterised by boat yards and beautifully preserved captains' villas.

Seafaring and fishing in the harsh North Atlantic is depicted in the *Fisheries Museum of the Atlantic (in summer daily 9.30am–5.30pm, winter until 5pm | admission C$12 | 68 Bluenose Dr.)*. A nice historic B & B in the centre of the village behind a shipyard is the ❊ INSIDER TIP *Pelham House (224 Pelham St. | tel. 902 634 7113 | www.pelhamhouse.ca | Budget)* with four rooms.

WHERE TO GO

KEJIMKUJIK NATIONAL PARK ★
(149 E6) (∅ N13)

The interior of Nova Scotia is an hour's drive from Lunenburg with idyllic lakes and rivers – ideal for swimming, camping and canoeing. Accommodation and canoe rental tip: *Whitman Inn (9 rooms | Caledonia | tel. 902 6 82 22 26 | www.whitmaninn.com | Budget)*.

PRINCE EDWARD ISLAND

(149 E–F4) (∅ N–O11)   Red potato fields, fine sandy beaches and well-kept cottages of the fishermen and farmers – this is one of the lasting impressions of this island that all visitors will take home with them.

The green island on the southern edge of the Gulf of St Lawrence with a length of 200 km/124 mi and a width of 60 km/37.3 mi is Canada's smallest province. Due to its bay-lined coast, the Prince Edward Island or *P.E.I.* (as it is usually abbreviated) has almost 800 km/497 mi of beaches. Because the sea reaches temperatures of over 20°C/68°F in summer, the island is a

Sea travel meets the Good Life: Café of the Fisheries Museum of the Atlantic in Lunenburg

preferred holiday destination for many Canadians. The fast Northumberland Strait car ferry connects the island to the port of *Pictou* and there is now (since 1998) also a bridge, the massive 12.9 km/8 mi long *Confederation Bridge* stretching from the mainland at *Cape Tormentine* in New Brunswick to *Borden* on P.E.I. There are four signposted ✂ scenic routes that will take you – mostly on idyllic back roads – to all the regions of the island.

The proud claim of P.E.I. is that it has the best lobster in Canada. This is something that you should ascertain for yourself in one of the many seafood restaurants or during a traditional ★ lobster supper. These evenings are however, not the elegant, refined evenings you would expect, but are instead rather loud and rustic – and touristy, too. Supper is often served in a community hall or in a shed at the harbour and then

the menu is usually chowder followed by a large lobster with a coleslaw or macaroni salad, corn on the cob and dessert – nobody leaves hungry. The famous *Malpeque oysters*, which are bred in a shallow bay near *Malpeque*, are also very delicious.

SIGHTSEEING

BASIN HEAD FISHERIES MUSEUM
In a beautiful setting on the coast, there is a small aquarium and exhibitions about the fishing industry. *In summer daily 9.30am–4.45pm | admission C$4 | Hwy. 16 | Souris*

CHARLOTTETOWN
The capital of the province (pop. 33,000) was established by the French in 1720, and has preserved its charming small-town atmosphere. In the restored, historic *Old Charlottetown* there are a

number of magnificent townhouses that were once the homes of rich captains and merchants.

NORTHERN COAST

The most beautiful beaches lie without a doubt in the North: there are white sand ones in the region around *Souris*, and reddish sand ones in the *P.E.I. National Park* at Cavendish. Various bays and shallow lagoons around *Greenwich Interpretive Centre* are home to water birds and many migratory birds – more than 300 species have been spotted here.

FOOD & DRINK

INSIDER TIP ▶ THE DUNES ✪

Bistro with potter's studio in a modern glass and wood building. Regional fish and lamb dishes from organic farms are served. *Route 15 | Brackley Beach | tel. 902 6 72 25 86 | Moderate*

FISHBONE'S SEAFOOD GRILL

Oysters, mussels, lobster, fish – all served in the best location, in an old townhouse in the heart of Charlottetown. *136 Richmond St. | tel. 902 6 28 65 69 | Budget–Moderate*

LEONHARD'S ✪

German bread and pastries, great breakfast and lunch on the main shopping street in Charlottetown. And all is ecologically produced. *Daily 9am–5pm | 12 Great George St. | Budget*

NEW GLASGOW LOBSTER SUPPERS

Tradition for almost fifty years: the whole town helps to serve visitors with an evening of fish soup, mussels and lobster. *Route 258 | New Glasgow | tel. 902 9 64 28 70 | Moderate*

TOURS

OUTSIDE EXPEDITIONS

Kayak and cycling tours on the northern coast of the island. Rented bicycles available. *370 Harbourview Dr. | North Rustico | tel. 902 9 63 33 66 | getoutside.com*

WHERE TO STAY

RODD CHARLOTTETOWN

Comfortable historical hotel in the centre of Charlottetown. *115 rooms | 75 Kent St. | tel. 902 8 94 73 71 | roddvacations.com | Moderate–Expensive*

SHAW'S HOTEL

Stylish country inn and restaurant with beautiful cabins close to the beach. *34 rooms | Brackley Beach | tel. 902 6 72 20 22 | www.shawshotel.ca | Moderate–Expensive*

INSIDER TIP ▶ WEST POINT LIGHTHOUSE

B & B in an old, historic lighthouse. This is not only a good restaurant but a small museum too. *13 rooms | West Point | tel. 902 8 59 36 05 | www.westpointharmony.ca | Budget–Moderate*

INFORMATION

P.E.I. VISITOR SERVICES

6 Prince St. | Charlottetown | tel. 800 4 63 47 34 | www.tourismpei.com

ST ANDREWS

(149 D5) (*∅ M12*) **The peaceful harbour village (pop. 1900) on the Passamaquoddy Bay is only a stone's throw away from the American State of Maine and has been a very popular summer holiday destination for more than a hundred years.**

Fresh fruits and vegetables as far as the eye can see: Old City Market in Saint John

You will see picturesque old wooden houses lining *Water Street,* which features small shops and seafood restaurants. Saint Andrews is also a good base for whale watching tours or trips to *Deer Island*, *Campobello Island* and *Grand Manan Island*. The *Algonquin Hotel (234 rooms | 184 Adolphus St. | tel. 506 5 29 88 23 | www.algonquinresort.com | Moderate–Expensive)* is a historic grand hotel with a large veranda, golf course and extensive garden.

SAINT JOHN

(149 D5) *(M12)* New Brunswick's largest city (pop. 126,000), at the mouth of the Saint John River in the Bay of Fundy, has one of Canada's most important harbours on the Atlantic, after Halifax.
The small old town at the river mouth has been restored and invites vistors to a stroll in the *Old City Market*. The *New Brunswick Museum (Mon–Fri 9am–5pm, Thu until 9pm, Sat 10am–5pm, Sun noon–5pm | admission C$10 | 1 Market Square | www.nbm-mnb.ca)* is the oldest museum in Canada and everything from the geology to the pioneer history of New Brunswick is represented here.

The city's biggest attraction is, however, the *Saint John River,* where tides cause the river to reverse its flow twice a day – during the high tide the sea water pushes inland. The phenomenon can be seen at the *Reversing Rapids (visitor centre)* – even from a zipline.

Find pure Victorian nostalgia in two renovated and lovingly furnished townhouses of the *Homeport Historic B & B (10 rooms | 80 Douglas Ave. | tel. 506 6 72 72 55 | www.homeport.ca | Moderate)*, which are located high above the Bay of Fundy.

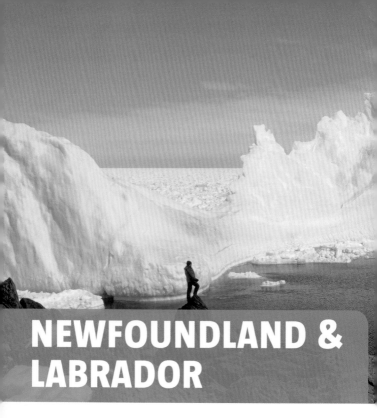

NEWFOUNDLAND & LABRADOR

Hospitality is a top priority in Newfoundland. Whether in the smaller towns or in the countless fishing villages – everywhere you will be welcomed with open arms.

Only a little over 500,000 people live on the island (about 42,000 mi²) with its majestic fjord landscape. The people here call their home 'the rock' – and there is indeed not much else other than sea and rocks. A thousand years ago the Vikings established a settlement at the northern tip of the current Newfoundland. Later, shortly after Columbus' journeys, John Cabot paved the way for the English, French, Basque and Portuguese who followed. Newfoundland only became a province of the State of Canada in 1949.

Labrador is the mainland part of the province: a wild almost completely unexplored world of lonely fjords and bays filled with icebergs – but also with legendary ore deposits, as demonstrated by the trove of nickel that was discovered in Voisey Bay in 1993. Only 27,000 people live here, scattered over almost 114,000 mi². The future might just be up here, which is one of the reasons why the Newfoundlanders have officially renamed the province *Newfoundland & Labrador*.

Newfoundlanders' major concern today is fishing. For four centuries they have lived off cod fishing on the once immensely rich Grand Banks, a continental shelf that stretches far into the Atlantic. John Cabot wrote that you need only

Photo: Icebergs off the Newfoundland rockbound coast

Fjords, mountains, cod – in the most isolated region of Canada things are done a little differently

'drop a bucket in the sea and it will fill up with fish'. But decades of overfishing have resulted in stocks declining dramatically and many factories have had to close.

The large oil discoveries off the east coast of the island (and tourism) have given residents some hope for the economy. Nature has created the perfect conditions: Newfoundland is ideal for hiking, kayaking, fishing and hunting. The island is easy to reach by plane or with the Marine Atlantic car ferries from Sydney in Nova Scotia *(6 hours passage | www.marineatlantic.ca)*. You can make a round trip on the Trans-Labrador Highway or travel by public ferry in summer further north to Nain.

The Newfoundlanders' accent and life-style often make them the target of jokes in other parts of Canada. But the *Newfies* have a sense of humour and bear their fate in a laid-back manner. A collection of typical jokes and more information about the island can be found at *upalong.org*.

L'ANSE AUX MEADOWS

(151 E1) (🗺 Q7) ● **In 1960 the fabled Viking colony, the Vinland, was discovered at the extreme northern tip of Newfoundland – the first settlement site of Europeans in the New World.**

Gros Morne National Park: a great chance to 'shoot' a moose

Eric the Red from Greenland came here in 1000 BC. The *National Historic Site (during the summer daily 9am–6pm | admission C$12)* has faithfully reconstructed earth huts and exhibitions (in the visitor centre) that illustrate the harsh life of the Norsemen. By far the best restaurant in the north of the island is the *Norseman Cafe.* Speciality: chowder, fish and lobster. They also have an art gallery and the *Valhalla B & B (7 rooms | tel. 709 7 54 31 05 | www.valhalla-lodge.com | Moderate).*

GROS MORNE NAT. PARK

(151 D2–3) (🗺 Q8) **The 700 mi² park is now a Unesco World Heritage Site; the park preserves the geologically unique west coast of Newfoundland with its fjords and mesas.**
The *Discovery Centre* in *Woody Point* explains the natural history of the park. A ★ *boat trip on the Western Brook Pond (reservations tel. 709 4 58 20 16 | www. bontours.ca),* a 15 km/9.3 mi long inland fjord, takes you past 600 m/1969 ft high cliffs. A 45-minute walk takes you to the lake and there are often moose along the way. Other boat trips are also available to *Bonne Bay* and the beautiful *Bay of Islands* further south.

LABRADOR

(0) (🗺 M–Q 1–6) **Covering a mainland area of around 116,000 mi², this province is truly one of the last wilderness areas on earth; it is only since the completion of Highway 510 a few years ago that a round trip on Labrador is possible.** Take the ferry to *Blanc Sablon,* then drive by car via *Cartwright* to *Goose Bay,* where you connect to the Québec road network. On the northern coast a car ferry travels to the Inuit village of *Nain,* the springboard for tours to the *Torngat Mountains National Park.*

SIGHTSEEING

BATTLE HARBOUR ★ ●

Bare rocks, colourful fishermen's houses and icebergs: the 250-year-old harbour town was once a centre for the cod fishery sector. *Boat tours from Mary's Harbour | www.battleharbour.com*

RED BAY

A fishing village situated somewhat further to the west that was once the site of the first Basque whaling station. The Basque sailed across the Atlantic around 1500, possibly even before Columbus.

ST JOHN'S

(151 F4) (*∅ S9*) **The capital of the province of Newfoundland & Labrador (pop. 210,000) is one of the oldest cities in North America and lies in a protected bay on the southeast coast of the island.**

The English and the French fought over the year-round ice-free natural harbour in the 17th century; today the harbour determines the life of the city – especially on *Water Street*.

SIGHTSEEING

CABOT TOWER/SIGNAL HILL

The first radio contact to Europe was made in 1901 from the tower that overlooks the harbour. The best views are from the 160 m/525 ft ☼ ● *Signal Hill*, especially in the morning. *Exhibition inside. In summer daily 10am–6pm, otherwise closed | admission C$4*

FLUVARIUM

Interesting ecological exhibitions with a stream that can be viewed through underwater windows. *During the summer Mon–Fri 9am–5pm, Sat/Sun from 10am| admission C$8 | Pippy Park*

INSIDER TIP ▶ JOHNSON GEO CENTRE

The mostly underground science museum explains the fascinating geology of Newfoundland. There is also a special exhibition on the tragic fate of the 'Titanic' that went down only 500 km/311 mi from here in the North Atlantic. *Daily 9.30am–5pm, winter closed on Mon | admission C$12 | 175 Signal Hill Rd. | www.geocentre.ca*

ST JOHN THE BAPTIST

Catholic cathedral built in 1841 with a richly decorated interior. *Daily 8am–4pm, Sat until 5pm, Son 8am–12.30pm | admission free| Military Rd.*

ST JOHN THE BAPTIST

The Anglican cathedral built in 1849 that bears the same name as the Catholic one. In July/August Wed–Sat afternoon tea and scones are served in the *Krypta*

★ **Boat trip on the Western Brook Pond**
Spectacular inland fjord with vertical cliffs glistening with foaming waterfalls
→ p. 100

★ **Battle Harbour**
An atmospheric journey into the world of the fishermen in the 19th century
→ p. 101

★ **Cape St Mary's**
High cliffs where massive colonies of seabirds nest closely together → p. 103

MARCO POLO HIGHLIGHTS

Tearoom (C$10). In summer daily 10am–4pm, Sat until noon | admission free | 16 Church Hill

THE ROOMS

Modern, very good provincial museum with exhibitions about pioneer history and the region's art and culture. Often special exhibitions by regional artists. *In summer Mon–Sat 10am–5pm, Wed until 9pm, Sun noon–5pm | admission C$10 | 9 Bonaventure Ave. | www.therooms.ca*

FOOD & DRINK

CLASSIC CAFÉ EAST

Hearty Newfoundland food: very good breakfast. You can sit out on the terrace in good weather. *73 Duckworth St. | tel. 709 726 44 44 | Budget–Moderate*

LOW BUDGET

The most impressive nature experience in Newfoundland is free of charge: iceberg watching. In spring and summer the white giants drift down from the Arctic on the Labrador Current. They are best seen from the coast at St Anthony and north of St John's as well as from the Twillingate headland. Satellite information about the position of the icebergs at *www.icebergfinder.com.*

The Rooms Café at the provincial museum in St John's serves affordable salads, and Newfoundland cuisine. Very good: the fish chowder *(daily breakfast and lunch, Wed also evenings)*. Admission to the museum is free on every first Wednesday evening of the month.

TRAPPER JOHN'S

Historically-styled pub, famous for its *screech-in* ceremony where visitors to the island are sworn in by kissing a cod (or a stuffed puffin) and then downing a shot of rum (screech). *2 George St. | Budget*

SHOPPING

In the shops along *Water Street* and *Duckworth Street* you will find souvenirs such as beautiful model ships, traditional knitted gloves and arts and crafts from remote villages.

TOURS

INSIDER TIP EAST COAST TRAIL

Spectacular 220 km/137 mi long trail along the east coast of the Avalon Peninsula from St John's towards the south *(www.eastcoasttrail.com).* Organised tours and baggage transport are offered by *Trail Connections (tel. 709 3 35 83 15 | www.trailconnections.ca).*

INSIDER TIP O'BRIENS BOAT TOURS

This place offers boat trips to the bird rocks and for whale watching. *Bay Bulls | tel. 709 7 53 48 50 | www.obriensboat tours.com*

WHERE TO STAY

MURRAY PREMISES

Small, elegant hotel right on the harbour in a renovated warehouse. *47 rooms | 5 Beck's Cove | tel. 709 7 38 77 73 | murray premiseshotel.com | Expensive*

QUALITY HOTEL

Modern and the best location in the town centre with a view of the harbour. Good restaurant. *160 rooms | 2 Hill O'Chips | tel. 709 7 54 77 88 | www.stjohnsqualityhotel. com | Moderate*

In the old days, everything was about fishing; today, Twillingate depends on tourism

INFORMATION

NEWFOUNDLAND & LABRADOR TOURISM
Info centres at the airport and at the City Hall | tel. 800 5 63 63 53 | www.new foundlandlabrador.com

WHERE TO GO

CAPE SPEAR ☆ **(151 F4)** *(ⅉ S9)*
This windblown headland is 10 km/6 mi from St John, it has a 19th century lighthouse and is the easternmost point of North America.

CAPE ST MARY'S ★ **(151 E5)** *(ⅉ S10)*
In the summer, huge colonies of gannets and gulls gather on the rocky headland about 150 km/93 mi southwest of St John's. ☆ From a high vantage point you will have a good view of the colony.

COLONY OF AVALON (151 F4) *(ⅉ S10)*
Ferryland, about 80 km/49.7 mi south of St John's, has excavations of the oldest English settlement in Newfoundland – established in 1621. You can join the archaeologists at work and see exhibitions on the history. *In summer daily 10am–6pm | admission C$11.30 | www. colonyofavalon.ca*

TWILLINGATE

(151 E2) *(ⅉ R8)* **A vast labyrinth of islands and bays surrounds the fishing village (pop. 2600).**
From April until early July you can also view INSIDERTIP massive icebergs from the ☆ *Long Point Lighthouse.* Worthwhile: a visit to the island of *Fogo* (car ferry) – also because of an art project with architecturally impressive studios for international artists *(www.shore fast.org).*

TOURS

TWILLINGATE ADVENTURE TOURS
Two-hour boat trip: icebergs, whales and sea lions in Notre Dame Bay. *tel. 709 8 84 59 99 | www.twillingate adventuretours.com*

DISCOVERY TOURS

1 EASTERN CANADA AT A GLANCE

START: 1 Toronto
END: 24 Halifax

19 days
Driving time
(without stops)
43 hours

Distance:
→ 3000 km/1864 mi

COSTS: approx. C$300 for petrol (car), for the boat tour to the 5 30 000 Islands CS$37 and for the admission to the performance in 17 Pays de la Sagouine CS$30–75

IMPORTANT TIPS: You can fly back from Halifax to Toronto or go by VIA-Rail – a good 24-hour panoramic trip.

All facets of Eastern Canada unfold along the route from the Great Lakes to the Atlantic. From the Niagara Falls to the cities, to the picturesque harbour town of

Would you like to explore the places that are unique to this region? Then the Discovery Tours are just the thing for you – they include terrific tips for stops worth making, breathtaking places to visit, selected restaurants and fun activities. It's even easier with the Touring App: download the tour with map and route to your smartphone using the QR Code on pages 2/3 or from the website address in the footer below – and you'll never get lost again even when you're offline.

TOURING APP

→ p. 2/3

Nova Scotia, the country shows its best – especially during the Indian Summer in early October. Don't be afraid of distances – there are hardly any traffic jams in Canada and drivers are relaxed and considerate.

You should take at least two days for ❶ Toronto → p. 32: take the time for a ride to the CN Tower, a stroll through the city, a shopping afternoon in Eaton Centre – and for all shoe fetishists a visit to the Bata Shoe Museum. After roughly a **two-hour trip on the Queen Elizabeth Way (QEW, Hwy 403)** you will reach the first highlight of the

DAY 1–3
❶ Toronto

130 km/81 mi

Photo: Indian Summer along the Highway 60

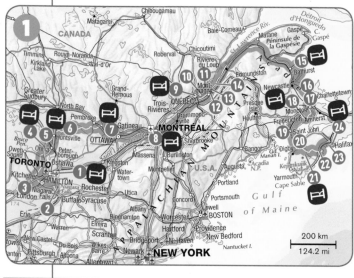

2 Niagara Falls
160 km/99 mi

route: the **2 Niagara Falls → p. 48**. The Niagara region provides, in addition to the massive falls, much enjoyment of life in the form of excellent vineyards such as the **INSIDER TIP Reif Winery** *(daily 10am–6pm | 156089 Niagara Parkway | reifwinery.com)*. An afternoon here passes in no time.

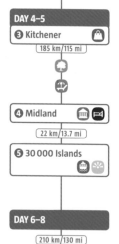

DAY 4–5

3 Kitchener
185 km/115 mi

4 Midland
22 km/13.7 mi

5 30 000 Islands

Travel back through old German settlements near **3 Kitchener → p. 42** with its large farmer's markets that are held on Saturdays. You will head **north and travel on country roads through fertile farmland to the shore of Georgian Bay**, a side bay of the vast Lake Huron. Do take the time for a swim: **Wasaga Beach** is a very popular and heavily visited in summer. The largest city on the lake is **4 Midland → p. 47**. A museum village and other historical sites remind of the Huron Indians, the glittering waters of Georgian Bay invite you to a boat trip in the region of **5 30 000 Islands**, e.g. with the **Miss Midland** *(177 King St. | tel. 1705 5 49 33 88 | www.midlandtours.com)*. It is said that this was the place where the Group of Seven painters found their inspiration for their art.

DAY 6–8
210 km/130 mi

Next you will travel through the classically Canadian Muskoka region, which is characterized by lakes and forests. Follow **Hwy. 11** until you get to Huntsville and then the route will follow **Hwy. 60** through the wooded area of the ⑥ **Algonquin Provincial Park** → p. 45, one of the most beautiful parks in Ontario. The secluded lakes are perfect for a canoe trip. If you want it more lively, book a full-day rafting trip on the rather wild Ottawa River east of the provincial park, such as from **Owl Rafting** *(price C$ 115–135 | tel. 1800 4 61 72 38 | Forester Falls | www. owl-mkc.ca)*. From here it is **only a few hours trip on the Trans-Canada Highway** and you will get to the well-kept capital of Canada, ⑦ **Ottawa** → p. 51. It is well worth spending a full day in the capital as this city has excellent museums and colourful neighbourhoods around the By-ward Market with its lovely cafes.

Then continue **on the Trans-Canada Highway in the Province of Québec** to the distinctively French metropolises of Canada. Expect an urban culture in the metropolis of ⑧ **Montréal** → p. 58. The best way to experience their French-Canadian esprit is to stroll around Boulevard St-Denis and to the Marché Jean Talon. You should not miss this: shopping is a pleasure on Rue Ste-Catherine and in the Ville Souterraine. Then you have to **drive for nearly three hours on Hwy 20 to the provincial capital** of ⑨ **Québec City** → p. 75, which will stun Europeans with its medieval centre that is fully encompassed by town walls – and last but not least with all its old French charm. You will get a good impression of Québec's picturesque countryside on a day trip by boat to the ⑩ **Île d'Orléans** → p. 81 and the historic ⑪ **Côte de Beaupré** → p. 81 along **Route 138 on the north bank of the river**.

The trip **downstream along the south shore of St Lawrence River is quick on Hwy 20** – but do make detours to the old French pioneer villages of **Gaspésie** → p. 72 such as ⑫ **Montmagny** and ⑬ **Cap-St-Ignace**, along the riverside road Route 132. In late summer, INSIDER TIP large flocks of snow geese gather in several bird reservoirs in the wide shore bank before migrating to the south. You should stop at the woodcarver city ⑭ **St-Jean-Port-Joli** → p. 72, where the traditional restaurant **La Bousti-faille** *(tel. 1 418 5 98 30 61 | 547, Rue de Gaspé Est | www. rocheaveillon.com | Moderate)* serves hearty Québec cuisine. **Route 132 climbs from Mont-Joli across the Chic Choc mountains of Gaspésie eastward to the Baie de Chaleur and the province of New Brunswick.** You will not

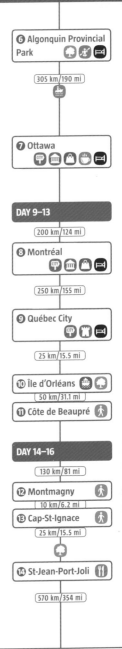

⑥ Algonquin Provincial Park

305 km / 190 mi

⑦ Ottawa

DAY 9–13

200 km / 124 mi

⑧ Montréal

250 km / 155 mi

⑨ Québec City

25 km / 15.5 mi

⑩ Île d'Orléans

50 km / 31.1 mi

⑪ Côte de Beaupré

DAY 14–16

130 km / 81 mi

⑫ Montmagny

10 km / 6.2 mi

⑬ Cap-St-Ignace

25 km / 15.5 mi

⑭ St-Jean-Port-Joli

570 km / 354 mi

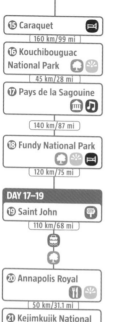

⑮ Caraquet

`160 km/99 mi`

⑯ Kouchibouguac National Park

`45 km/28 mi`

⑰ Pays de la Sagouine

`140 km/87 mi`

⑱ Fundy National Park

`120 km/75 mi`

DAY 17–19

⑲ Saint John

`110 km/68 mi`

⑳ Annapolis Royal

`50 km/31.1 mi`

㉑ Kejimkujik National Park

be disappointed if you continue along the Atlantic coast: **Hwy. 11 will lead you through the old settlement land of the Acadians nearby ⑮ Caraquet** → p. 88 and further to the **⑯ Kouchibouguac National Park** → p. 93, which is a quiescent dune landscape on the Atlantic. The cultural centre in **Bouctouche** is built on an island and called **⑰ Pays de la Sagouine** *(57 Acadie St. | tel. 1506 7 43 14 00 | www.sagouine.com)*. It uses theatrical performances to show what life in an Acadian fishing village was like a hundred years ago. **Hwys 15 and 114 continue via Moncton to the Bay of Fundy**. The next big attraction is again an experience of nature: the mighty tides in the **⑱ Fundy National Park** → p. 90 – 12 m/40 ft tidal range!

The visit to **⑲ Saint John** → p. 97 is followed by a short **ferry ride across the Bay of Fundy** and you will have reached the large peninsula of Nova Scotia. Scallops and lobster are local specialities – and they are available everywhere in the many restaurants of the province, which is a very popular summer vacation spot. In the historic village **⑳ Annapolis Royal** → p. 85 the Canadian-Austrian Restaurant **Compose** *(235 Saint George St. | tel. 1902 5 32 12 51 | Moderate)* serves this seafood with a wonderful view across the water. **Continue on Hwy. 8** and active holiday makers can take a canoe trip in the many lakes of the **㉑ Kejimkujik National**

Everybody visiting Nova Scotia eventually drives to the lighthouse of Peggy's Cove

Park → p. 94. You will then **continue on Hwys 208 and 325** to the attractive ports of the south coast. These could be locations such as ㉒ **Lunenburg** → p. 94 and the postcard-like village ㉓ **Peggy's Cove** → p. 93 before the route **via Hwy. 3** ends in the lively nightlife of ㉔ **Halifax**.

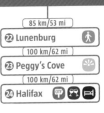

| 85 km/53 mi |
| ㉒ Lunenburg |
| 100 km/62 mi |
| ㉓ Peggy's Cove |
| 100 km/62 mi |
| ㉔ Halifax |

② BOLD CLIFFS AND SANDY BEACHES: THE ATLANTIC COAST

START: ❶ Halifax	13 days
END: ❶ Halifax	Driving time (without stops)
Distance: ⊙ 3000 km/1864 mi	42 hours

COSTS: approx. C$300 for petrol (cars), car ferry to ❽ **Prince Edward Island** approx. C$75, rafting on the ⑰ **Shubenacadie River** C$70–100, canoe rental in ⑲ **Kejimkujik National Park** C$43–70

WHAT TO PACK: Raincoat, swimming suit

IMPORTANT TIPS: Best travel time: June to end of August and in early October. Some restaurants and B & Bs close for winter in early September already despite the fact that visitors come for Indian Summer.

A tour through the Atlantic provinces of Canada is a trip to picturesque fishing villages, lobster restaurants and stormy water cliffs in Nova Scotia, to forests and tranquil mudflats in New Brunswick and to the amazingly warm (in summer) dune beaches on Prince Edward Iceland.

Start at ❶ **Halifax** → p. 90, from where **Hwy. 7 winds eastward along the flat south coast of Nova Scotia with its countless bays.** There will be long rows of white buoys in the dark water, which indicate that oysters are being farmed around the fishing villages. Small farms in the area try to grow some vegetables in the barren ground. Pioneer life of some 150 years ago along this coastline must have been much more difficult – and lonesome – as documented by the museum village ❷ **Sherbrooke Village** (June–Oct daily 9.30am–5pm | admission C$13.75 | on Hwy. 7)

On the other side of the dam across the 1.5 km/0.9 mi wide and 65 m/215 ft deep Strait of Canso awaits a highlight of the trip to conclude the first day: ❸ **Cape Breton Island** → p. 86 with the National Park of the same

| **DAY 1–4** |
| ❶ Halifax |
| 200 km/124 m |
| ❷ Sherbrooke Village |
| 110 km/68 mi |
| ❸ Cape Breton Island |

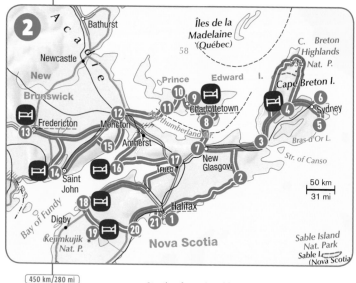

name. Starting from the old French fishing village **Chéti-camp**, the **magnificent panoramic road of the Cabot Trail** leads around the park. An ideal location to stay is ❹ **Bad-deck**. You should plan some island explorations for the next three days. This could be a walk along the almost 10 km/6.2 mi long **Skyline Trail** in the National Park and a whale watching tour that start from Chéticamp. Delicious ice cream is sold in small shops that will tempt you again and again – it is a passion of the local people. And do not miss a day's visit to the beautifully restored Old French co-lonial town ❺ **Forteresse de Louisbourg → p. 87 on the southeast tip of Cape Breton**. Equally fascinating: **About an hour's drive further to the north is the mining town Glace Bay**. The ❻ INSIDER TIP **Miners' Museum** *(in sum-mer daily 10am–6pm | admission C$13 | 42 Birkley St.)* shows how coal was mined previously in miles and miles of tunnels that were built under the sea.

The way back from the island leads through lush green farmland. **It continues through the northern part of Nova Scotia on the Trans-Canada Highway. You will pass the old Scottish settlements Antigonish, New Glasgow and** ❼ **Pictou**, a busy harbour village of lobster fishermen, whose work is explained in the **Northumberland Fisher-ies Museum** *(in summer daily 10am–6pm | admission C$6 |*

---

450 km/280 mi

❹ Baddeck

115 km/71 mi

❺ Forteresse de Louisbourg

55 km/34.2 mi

❻ Miners' Museum

DAY 5–7

210 km/130 mi

❼ Pictou

Skyline Trail: you start out through the forest and then go up to the cliffs with the best views

71 Front St.). You will also get acquainted with mini lobster and even adopt one when you find out about lobster breeding. In mid-July is **Lobster Carnival**. **The next goal is a just a short ferry ride away:** the idyllic island province **⑧ Prince Edward Island** → p. 94. It is famous for its wonderful sandy beaches such as the INSIDER TIP **Panmure Beach** **on the East Coast that is just an hour's drive away from the ferry terminal.** Then there is the tiny capital that you should definitely visit: **⑨ Charlottetown** → p. 95. Then you should treat yourself to a two-day break: swim near the red shimmering sands of **⑩ Prince Edward Island National Park**, take a bike ride along the coast – and feast on lobster in the fishing villages such as **North Rustico**. The island is small, so you can rent a room for three nights near the National Park or the centre of Charlottetown, e.g. in the **Hillhurst Inn** *(8 rooms | 181 Fitzroy St. | tel. 1 902 8 92 50 22 | Moderate).*

The massive ⑪ Confederation Bridge, completed in 1998, leads for 13 km/8.1 mi high above the waves of the Northumberland Strait back to the mainland – to Cape Tormentine in the very south of the Province of New Brunswick. Expansive marsh landscapes accompany the **trip via Shediac to ⑫ Moncton**, where you will find a rare natural phenomenon: Due to the tidal difference of 7.5 m/25 ft,

40 km/24.9 mi

⑧ Prince Edward Island

110 km/68 mi

⑨ Charlottetown

35 km/21.8 mi

⑩ Prince Edward Island National Park

80 km/49.7 mi

DAY 8–9

⑪ Confederation Bridge

100 km/62 mi

⑫ Moncton

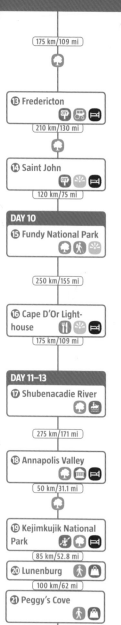

175 km/109 mi

⑬ Fredericton

210 km/130 mi

⑭ Saint John

120 km/75 mi

DAY 10

⑮ Fundy National Park

250 km/155 mi

⑯ Cape D'Or Lighthouse

175 km/109 mi

DAY 11–13

⑰ Shubenacadie River

275 km/171 mi

⑱ Annapolis Valley

50 km/31.1 mi

⑲ Kejimkujik National Park

85 km/52.8 mi

⑳ Lunenburg

100 km/62 mi

㉑ Peggy's Cove

the flow of the Petitcodiac River reverses twice a day. You can often observe a 30–40 cm/12–16 in high tidal bore, when the salt water runs against the river. But do not underestimate the inland, as it has its charms too: Gentle hills, forests and farms accompany the **Trans-Canada Highway 2 to the provincial capital ⑬ Fredericton → p. 89** with the nostalgic museum village **Kings Landing**. Continue through the idyllic valley of the Saint John River on **Hwy. 102 south to the Bay of Fundy and the historical commercial town ⑭ Saint John → p. 97**, which hold an unusual phenomenon: the tidal range in the harbour reverses the rapids in the stream.

You have to go further east **via Hwy. 1 and Hwy. 114** to see the record-setting tidal range **in the ⑮ Fundy National Park → p. 90.** A height difference of 12 m/39.4 ft has been measured. What a great opportunity for a walk on the seabed – but be sure to keep a close eye on the tidal schedule. **Continue via Moncton to Trans-Canada Highway 2.** A nice detour beyond the tourist-beaten path is a **two-hour drive south-west of Sackville**. The restaurant in the ⑯ **Cape D'Or Lighthouse** offers great fish dishes with a spectacular view across the Bay of Fundy. There are simple rooms in the guest house of the lighthouse if you with to stay longer in the evening.

Once back in Nova Scotia, take Hwys 236 and 215 from Truro and you quickly reach the ⑰ Shubenacadie River for an unusual and very wet rafting experience. You can ride the river's turbulent tidal for 18 km/11.2 mi upstream: INSIDER TIP **Tidal Bore Rafting Park & Cottages** (12215 Hwy. 215 | Urbania | tel. 1902 758 84 33 | www.raftingcanada.ca). The route then follows the Fundy Coast **via the Hwys. 215, 101 and 1 westward into the ⑱ Annapolis Valley**. A valley steeped in history, because this is where the first Frenchmen settled in Canada in 1604 at **Port Royal**. South of **Annapolis Royal → p. 85**, **Hwy. 8 leads through hilly woodland.** In the ⑲ **Kejimkujik National Park → p. 94** you will have the opportunity to experience Canada in a classic way: in a canoe on one of the placid lakes. There will be more hustle and bustle on the **way back to Halifax along the South Coast**: The picturesque harbour villages in the region, such as ⑳ **Lunenburg → p. 94, Mahone Bay** or ㉑ **Peggy's Cove → p. 93**, do earn their main living today from tourism. So it is no surprise that you will find many galleries and handicraft shops, but you will also find excellent places for a fare-well dinner with fresh fish or lobster before returning to **❶ Halifax**.

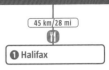

45 km/28 mi

❶ Halifax

❸ ALONG ST LAWRENCE RIVER THROUGH NEW FRANCE

START: ❶ Montréal END: ❶ Montréal	**11 days** Driving/ferry time (without stops) **50 hours**
Distance: 🚗 2900 km/1802 mi	

COSTS: approx. C$300 for petrol (cars), whale watching tour from ⑪ Tadoussac C$72–85

IMPORTANT TIPS: Nice in summer, but the trip is most impressive during the Indian Summer in early October.

The common thread of this journey through the 'Belle Province' is the St Lawrence River, the historical river of New France. Its shores are lined with colourful cities and old settler villages, and in the surrounding forests you have the Laurentian Mountains and the cliff-lined Gaspé Peninsula.

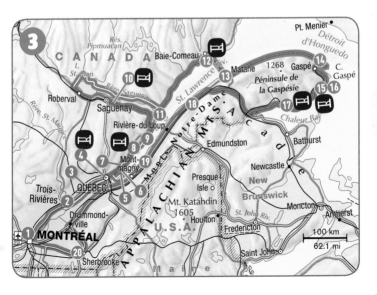

Sometimes you only get to see dolphins, but whale-watching tours still remain very popular.

DAY 1–3

❶ Montréal

140 km/87 mi

❷ Trois-Rivières

65 km/40.4 mi

❸ Deschambault

60 km/37.3 mi

❹ Québec City

25 km/15.5 mi

❺ Île d'Orléans

85 km/52.8 mi

DAY 4–5

❻ Beaupré

5 km/3.1 mi

❼ Parc du Mont Ste-Anne

From the lively metropolis **❶ Montréal** → p. 58, take **Hwy. 40 through the fertile lowlands of the St Lawrence River** to **❷ Trois-Rivières** → p. 83 with its charming historic old town. **For the next section follow Route 138** on the north bank of the river that by now has reached a massive width of several hundred yards. The winding country road will now follow the old *Chemin du Roi*, which the then governor of New France had built in 1737 to connect the settlements of the farmers with the large estates of the aristocrats. You will see mansions, magnificent old churches and mills built in the Norman style in small places like **❸ Deschambault** or **Portneuf** that are reminiscent of the heydays of *Nouvelle France*. And just a little further 'down the road' you will get to the listed historic centre of **❹ Québec City** → p. 75 and, ahead of the city, the island **❺ Île d'Orléans** → p. 81 with its nostalgic farmers villages. There is plenty of historical flair.

Also **the next section follows the north shore of St Laurent River**: along the Côte de Beaupré → p. 81 to the old pilgrimage destination **❻ Beaupré** and **❼ Parc du Mont Ste-Anne** *(mont-sainte-anne.com | www.canyonsa.qc.ca)*. Get physically active and get your pulse racing at a fantastic zip-line at a height of 60 m/196.9 ft. Or maybe you prefer heights and want to indulge in some paragliding

or canyoning? **Then you continue on Route 138 to ⑧ Baie-Saint-Paul → p. 70**. Treat yourself to a night in the stylish hotel **Le Germain Charlevoix** *(145 rooms | tel. 1418 2 40 41 20 | www.legermain hotels.com | Moderate)*, which is part of an ecological project of the creative (and very rich) founder of Cirque du Soleil. Highly recommended: an afternoon in the hotel's luxurious spa. The winding **Route 362 on the high bank of the stream offers great views and leads to the beautifully situated artist village ⑨ La Malbaie and Route 170** takes you to the mountains: to the almost 'Norwegian' looking fjords of the ⑩ **Saguenay Region → p. 82** and to lake **Lac Saint-Jean**. Old industrial places like **Chicoutimi** – a stronghold of Québec separatists – alternate with sleepy villages, rugged high banks and beaches on the lake. Don't leave without trying the region's blueberry pie, such as in Saint-Felicien in the **Pâtisserie Chez Gran-Maman** *(1883, Blvd. du Jardin | tel. 1418 6 79 55 51 | Budget)*.

Keep your eyes open when you **continue on Route 172 and Route 138**, because you can often observe belugas and other whales at the mouth of the rivers Saguenay and St Lawrence – the experience is most impressive when you see them on a 2–3 hour boat ride from ⑪ **Tadoussac**, for instance with **Otis Excursion** *(431, Bateau-Passeur | tel. 1418 2 35 41 97 | www.otisexcursions.com)*. On the route to the small town ⑫ **Baie-Comeau → p. 70** you will get many great views across the St Lawrence River. The mountains push closer to the coast, the landscape becomes lonelier and the land gets a harsh Nordic touch.

The journey by car ferry leads to the south bank of the St Lawrence River that almost looks like a bay by now. The target port Matane is already on the scenic peninsula ⑬ **Gaspésie → p. 72, which is mostly surrounded by Route 132 along the coast**. The scenic route reaches its dramatic climax in ⑭ **Parc National de Forillon**.

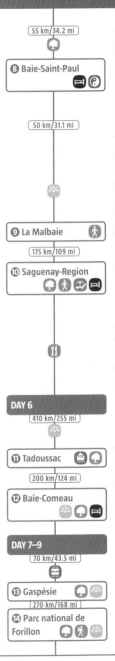

55 km/34.2 mi

⑧ Baie-Saint-Paul

50 km/31.1 mi

⑨ La Malbaie

175 km/109 mi

⑩ Saguenay-Region

DAY 6

410 km/255 mi

⑪ Tadoussac

200 km/124 mi

⑫ Baie-Comeau

DAY 7–9

70 km/43.5 mi

⑬ Gaspésie

270 km/168 mi

⑭ Parc national de Forillon

Beautiful: the simple 8 km/5 mi long hike along **Les Graves**. Pebble beaches alternate with steep cliffs and wooded areas on the way to the lighthouse of **Cap Gaspé**. You should stay a day at the village ⑮ **Percé**: take a walk on the beach and a boat trip to the bird colonies of ⑯ **Île Bonaventure** → p. 74. Sunny resorts on the ⑰ **Baie des Chaleurs** line the distant route around the peninsula.

You will now stay on Route 132 for a while as you head back west to the valley of the St Lawrence River. Something very interesting along the way: the ⑱ **Parc national du Bic** near Rimouski and the wood carving village ⑲ **St-Jean-Port-Joli** → p. 72. You should detour from the highway **on Route 20 on your way back from Québec City to Montréal: On Route 55 south toward Magog → p. 72** lies the farmland of ⑳ **Eastern Townships** that was originally populated by the British, with forest-encircled lakes and small idyllic villages like **North Hatley**. It is worthwhile taking the time to make this detour as it makes for an agreeable end to this fascinating tour before you **take Route 10 to head back to** ❶ **Montréal**.

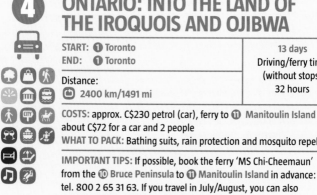

4 ONTARIO: INTO THE LAND OF THE IROQUOIS AND OJIBWA

START: ❶ Toronto	13 days
END: ❶ Toronto	Driving/ferry time
Distance:	(without stops)
🖥 2400 km/1491 mi	32 hours

COSTS: approx. C$230 petrol (car), ferry to ⑪ Manitoulin Island about C$72 for a car and 2 people
WHAT TO PACK: Bathing suits, rain protection and mosquito repellent

IMPORTANT TIPS: If possible, book the ferry 'MS Chi-Cheemaun' from the ⑩ Bruce Peninsula to ⑪ Manitoulin Island in advance: tel. 800 2 65 31 63. If you travel in July/August, you can also experience the pow-wow celebrations of the Iroquois.

The contrasts between bustling towns and wild nature make the second largest province in Canada especially appealing. You have Toronto and the elegant city of Ottawa, the lonely lakes of Algonquin Provincial Park, the thundering Niagara Falls and the rocky shores of Lake Huron, and last but not least the Indian reservations, such as on Manitoulin Iceland.

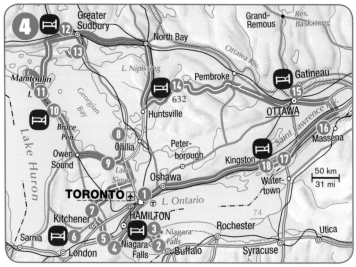

From **①** **Toronto** → p. 32 you only have to travel **130 km/81 mi on the motorway Queen Elizabeth Way (Hwy 403)** before you reach Ontario's most famous attraction: **②** **Niagara Falls** → p. 48. From there you continue on side roads: **on the Niagara Parkway to the historic town ③** **Niagara-on-the-Lake** → p. 51 with wineries such as **Peller Winery** *(tasting and gourmet restaurant; in summer open daily, Mon–Thu 10am–9pm, Fr–Sun 9am–10pm | 290 John St. E | www.peller.com)*.

The route leads through the orchards of St Catharines into the land of the Iroquois to the ④ **Six Nations Reserve near Ohsweken**, where pow-wow celebrations are held at the end of July and at the end of August. You can buy Native American art at **Iroqrafts** *(1880 Tuscarora Rd. | www.iroqrafts.com)*. **Next door in ⑤** **Brantford**, the excellent Museum of the **INSIDERTIP** **Woodland Cultural Centre** *(Mon–Fri 9am–4pm, Sat 10am–5pm | admission C$7 | 184 Mohawk St. | www.sixnationstourism.ca)* shows the history of Canada – from the perspective of the Native Americans. **Stroll on Hwy. 24 and Hwy. 8** into the old city of the Germans in Canada: **⑥** **Kitchener** → p. 42. The farmland around the city is mainly settled by Mennonites who sell their own products on the very large farmer's market in **⑦** **St Jacobs** → p. 43.

DAY 1–2
① Toronto
130 km/81 mi
② Niagara Falls
25 km/15.5 mi
③ Niagara-on-the-Lake
110 km/68 mi
④ Six Nations Reserve
25 km/15.5 mi
⑤ Brantford
50 km/31.1 mi
⑥ Kitchener
20 km/12.4 mi
⑦ St. Jacobs

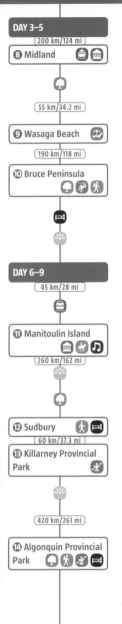

DAY 3–5

200 km/124 mi

⑧ Midland

55 km/34.2 mi

⑨ Wasaga Beach

190 km/118 mi

⑩ Bruce Peninsula

DAY 6–9

45 km/28 mi

⑪ Manitoulin Island

260 km/162 mi

⑫ Sudbury

60 km/37.3 mi

⑬ Killarney Provincial Park

420 km/261 mi

⑭ Algonquin Provincial Park

Continue your journey on country roads: **via Elora to Hwy. 400 and north to Georgian Bay at Lake Huron**. **⑧ Midland** → p. 47 was once an important settlement centre of the Huron tribe. Worthwhile: a boat trip to **30 000 Islands** and a trip to the suburb **Penetanguishene**, where the museum village **Discovery Harbour** → p. 126 shows the life of the white soldiers and settlers from 200 years ago. Sunbathers will rather prefer the beaches of **⑨ Wasaga Beach** → p. 48 and **Collingwood**. **Then take Hwys. 92, 26 and 6 westwards along the Georgian Bay**. It's time to stop for a day: At the tip of the **⑩ Bruce Peninsula** in the national park with the same name you will find in **Tobermory** quiet bays with crystal clear water and trails along the rocky coastline begging to be discovered – and for divers there are exciting wreck dives. Great for one night with a view of the sea: the **Grandview Motel** *(8 rooms | tel. 1519 5 96 22 20 | Moderate)* in Tobermory.

A short ferry ride with the 'MS Chi-Cheemaun' takes you north to ⑪ Manitoulin Island → p. 47, the island of the Ojibwa Indians. In the museum **Ojibwe Cultural Foundation** *(www.ojibweculture.ca)* in West Bay you will learn details about the culture of the tribes, on the **Kicking Mule Ranch** *(Hwy. 6 | tel. 1705 8 59 12 34 | www.manitoulin-island.com/kmr)* you can go horseback riding in the woods – and dances will be held on many weekends during the summer. **Hwy. 6 leads through a wild-romantic landscape further north to the mainland and then, through lonely forests on the Trans-Canada Highway, to the mining town ⑫ Sudbury** → p. 57. Tip for wildlife fans: take a (multi-day) canoe trip in the still largely untouched **⑬ Killarney Provincial Park** south of the town (boat hire available on Hwy 637).

Continue on the Trans-Canada Highway to North Bay on the shores of Lake Nipissing and then south to Huntsville. For a whole day, the route runs through the typical landscape of the Canadian Shield – forests, lakes, granite rocks, as far as the eye can see. The scenery is quite similar **on Hwy. 60 in the ⑭ Algonquin Provincial Park** → p. 45, where you can observe – with a relatively high probability – moose and beaver along the trails or on a canoe trip. This is what you picture Canada to be like! Park the car for a day, hire a canoe at **Opeongo Lake**, the largest lake in Algonquin Park, and discover the wilderness. If you rather prefer it to be comfortable, you can have the canoe transported for you some distance into the hinterland by water taxi. Route advice, canoeing and camping gear are available directly at the lake from **Opeongo Store & Water Taxi** *(reservations under tel. 1613 6 37 20 75 | www.algonquin outfitters.com)*. PS: You will find many beautiful camping sites along the lakefront for overnight trips.

In the broad valley of the Ottawa River things become more civilised once again: small farms, apple orchards and vegetable fields line **Hwy. 17 to the federal capital** ⑮ **Ottawa → p. 51**. You should spend a day there as the city has excellent museums and beautiful promenades. **Follow Hwys. 417 and 138 to Cornwall** into the valley of the St Lawrence River and, on the bank of the river, follow the idyllic **panoramic route of the Long Sault Parkway to** ⑯ **Morrisburg → p. 55** and the museum village **Upper Canada Village**. The last part of the route runs **along the broad St Lawrence River through the scenic island world of** ⑰ **Thousand Islands** (boat trips are available from Gananoque) to the historic university city ⑱ **Kingston → p. 46** and then **take Highway 401 on the north shore of Lake Ontario back to** ❶ **Toronto**.

DAY 10–13

285 km/177 mi

⑮ Ottawa

140 km/87 mi

⑯ Morrisburg

100 km/62 mi

⑰ Thousand Islands

40 km/24.9 mi

⑱ Kingston

260 km/162 mi

❶ Toronto

A good museum on Manitoulin Island informs about the culture of the Ojibwa

SPORTS & ACTIVITIES

Be it traditional activities such as canoeing, golf or tennis or more trendy sports such as sea kayaking and mountain biking – the Canadians are enthusiastic. Thanks to the pioneers, the outdoor life is in their blood. And nature offers them – often even in the direct environs of the large cities – the very best opportunities for their sport. It is also made easy for visitors as every major hotel and every holiday resort has their own fitness centre as well as an activity desk, where you can book tee-off times for the on-site golf course and obtain information about other activities on offer in the area.

Several rental shops in parks and cities rent out canoes, bicycles and other sporting equipment – along with tips and maps. Organised day tours can also be booked on the spot or on short notice. Cycling, diving or kayaking excursions that are several days long are best booked in advance.

CANOE & KAYAK TRIPS

Trekking through the wilderness just like the Native Americans and trappers once did is one of the most beautiful experiences in Canada. Canoes can be rented (hourly or daily) at many lodges and outfitters – and there are scenic lakes everywhere. Areas of true wilderness, where you can follow the footsteps of fur traders, can be found in northern Ontario. Sea kayaking is also popular in the sheltered bays on the Atlantic. For links

Active on water and on land: Eastern Canada's wide open spaces and scenic landscapes make it ideal for outdoor and sports enthusiasts

and tips on canoeing visit the website of the provincial parks in Ontario *(www. ontarioparks.com/paddling)*.

Good rafting trips are offered on the Ottawa River at Beachburg, west of Ottawa, e.g. with *Wilderness Tours (tel. 888 723 86 69 | www.wildernesstours.com)*. Canoe rentals and beautiful multi-day canoe trips with stays in a tent or cabin are offered in the west of Algonquin Park by *Voyageur Quest Lodge (Round Lake, Algonquin Park | tel. 416 4 86 36 05 | www. voyageurquest.com)*.

CYCLING

There are good routes for multi-day trips on Cape Breton Island, Prince Edward Island and the country roads in southern Ontario in the region around Kitchener. In Canada it is never a problem to rent a bicycle as there are rental companies in most cities. *(Prices: C$20–35 per day , C$70–175 per week)*.

MacQueen's (430 Queen St. | Charlottetown | tel. 902 3 68 24 53 | www.mac queens.com) has bicycles for hire and organises trips on P.E.I. Bicycle hire for trips on the waterfront in Toronto and to the Toronto Islands are offered by *Wheel Excitement (249 Queens Quay W | behind the Radisson Admiral Hotel | tel. 416 2 60 90 00 | www.wheelexcitement.ca)*. And on the ● *Cabot Trail* in Nova Scotia *Cabot Trail Adventures (299 Shore Rd. | South Harbour | tel. 902 3 83 25 52 | www. cabottrailoutdooradventures.com)* offers guided tours as well as bicycle hire.

DIVING

One would not imagine that Canada offers underwater adventure. However, its crystal clear waters offer the best dive conditions – but you must have some experience and will need a wetsuit (and sometimes even a dry suit) for the icy Atlantic waters. If you are up for it, you can look for lobsters in the rock crevices and explore shipwrecks. The coast of *Nova Scotia* (Sable Island was formerly known as the graveyard of the Atlantic) and the *Bruce Peninsula* in Lake Huron are excellent diving sites.

You can do a one or multi-day dive excursion to the wrecks of whaling ships off the coast of Newfoundland or go whale and iceberg watching with *Ocean Quest (17 Stanley's Lane | Conception Bay South | tel. 709 8 34 72 34 | www.ocean questadventures.com)* near St John's.
Info for divers on the Bruce Peninsula and surroundings at the Tobermory online visitors guide *(tobermory.com)*.

FISHING

Fishing in the many lakes and rivers is fairly straightforward but you still need a permit. Depending on the province and the permit period, fishing licences cost from C$1–25 (for a day) to C$150 (for the coveted Atlantic salmon sport fishing) and are available at sport shops and lodges. The respective national parks sell their licenses in their visitor centres. Fishing enthusiasts will find ideal spots in the deserted north of the provinces – numerous lakes where perch, whiting and gutsy pike are just waiting for the bait.

Halley's Camps – offering a selection of isolated fly-in lodges and various wilderness camps in the north-west of Ontario – is an ideal choice for passionate anglers *(Minaki | tel. 807 2 24 65 31 | www.halleyscamps.com)*. Also perfectly suitable for nature lovers and anglers is INSIDERTIP *Phare de Pointe-des-Monts (Pointe-des-Monts | tel. 418 9 39 23 32, 866 3 69 40 83 | www.pointe-des-monts. com):* here you will find simple log cabins on the romantic north shore of the St Lawrence, whale watching included.

HIKING

The largest selection of trails – signposted and well maintained – can be found in the national and provincial parks. The wardens in the respective visitor centres are more than happy to provide information about the best trails. Good networks are offered, for instance, on *Cape Breton Highlands*, the *Gaspésie Peninsula* and also the *Bruce Peninsula*. Outside of the parks hiking is often difficult – in Canada wilderness really does mean wilderness. The INSIDERTIP *Trans-Canada Trail*, the longest path in the world, leading straight through all provinces from Newfoundland to the Pacific coast, is completely new: individual stages of this route are highly suitable for hiking. *(Information: www.tctrail.ca)*.

RIDING

The large ranches are mainly in the west of Canada, but there are also opportunities

Canada offers an almost unlimited freedom to ride through untouched nature

to ride out into the countryside in the east. Watch out for the signposts of trail riding outfitters who often have their signs up on the highways.

You need not be an experienced horse rider to give it a try as they ride in the Western style on stable saddles, and the good-natured horses walk very obediently in a row.

beautiful, including the one in the Blue Mountains, were you can even dive into the steaming outdoor swimming pools in winter. A great tip for Montréal is the *AmeriSpa (www.amerispa.ca)* in the hotel Le Crystal with a grand view over the city. Further information: *www.lead ingspasofcanada.com* and *www.travel towellness.com*.

WELLNESS

The spa holiday trend started in the United States and the Canadians quickly followed suit. Today all major resort hotels have a spa with gym, sauna, swimming pool, massage and yoga studios and sometimes innovative treatments and techniques.

The Scandinavian-style spas of the ● *Scandinave Spa (www.scandinave.com)* chain in Ontario and Québec are very

WINTER FUN

Although the few ski slopes cannot compare to the powder snow of the Rockies, you can still take part in snowshoe hiking, sledding, ice fishing and snowmobiling at various winter sport centres. The following one is recommended: *Deerhurst Resort (1235 Deerhurst Dr. | Huntsville | tel. 705 789 64 11 | www.deerhurstresort. com)*, a winter lodge west of the Algonquin Provincial Park.

TRAVEL WITH KIDS

Just like the United States, Canada is also a very child-friendly country. The Canadians themselves travel with their offspring during the holiday months of July and August and the tourist infrastructure is geared to families.

In the restaurants there are children's menus and of course child seats. Most hotels offer children's beds and cots (sometimes at no extra cost) and at many motels there is a paddling pool for the little ones next to the main swimming pool. The resort hotels and even some museums also offer special childcare facilities in kids' camps. Holiday resorts and hotels also offer babysitters and as car seats are mandatory, car rental companies also provide them on request. Travelling to Canada with children from three to four years is

no problem, if you plan your time accordingly and take your children's needs into consideration. Canoeing, for instance, is a lot of fun and there are lakes around every corner. Water parks and trapper forts are there to be explored and many places have their own children's museum. Travelling in a mobile home is also very popular: the vehicle creates a familiar, consistent environment while the outdoors and camping offer real adventure, making a holiday in Canada with kids a success.

TORONTO

BLACK CREEK PIONEER VILLAGE
(146 C4) (*∅ E13*)
The museum village 30 km/18.6 mi north-west of Toronto illustrates how

Holidays in Canada are great for children: swims in the lakes by day, toasting marshmallows around the campfire by night

the pioneers lived. Hammering in the workshops, grazing cows and special activities for children. *Summer daily 10am–5pm, Sat/Sun from 11am, autumn/spring 11am–4pm | admission C$15, children C$11 | 1000 Murray Ross Parkway (close to Hwy. 400) | www. blackcreek.ca*

CENTREVILLE AMUSEMENT PARK
(146 C5) (*ⅢⅢ E13*)
Lovely for the little ones: first a trip to the island on a ferry, then a traditional amusement park. *Late May–early Sept daily from 10.30am | admission pass for all the rides C$35, family pass C$110 | Centre Island | www.centreisland.ca*

ONTARIO SCIENCE CENTRE
(146 C5) (*ⅢⅢ E13*)
Large technology museum with amazing experiments that you can even reproduce with your children. Particularly impressive: a steaming rainforest. *Mon–Fri 10am–4pm, Sat until 8pm, Sun until 5pm | admission C$22, children C$13 |*

North York | 770 Don Mills Rd. | www.ontariosciencecentre.ca

TORONTO ZOO (146 C5) (⌂ *E13*)
Riding on a camel? Or a 'zoo mobile' trip through the 700-acre terrain with over 5000 animals. For smaller children there is the *Discovery Zone* with a petting zoo and water park – and a fantastic polar bear enclosure. *In summer 9am–7pm, otherwise until 9.30am–4.30pm | admission C$29, children C$19 | Hwy. 401 | Meadowvale Rd. | www.torontozoo.com*

ONTARIO

CANADIAN CHILDREN'S MUSEUM
(147 E3) (⌂ *G12*)
The national children's museum, a part of the *Museum of Civilization,* has a fantastic array of child-orientated exhibitions about the word's many cultures. *Daily 9.30am–5pm, Thu until 8pm | admission C$20, children C$12, families C$50 | 100, Rue Laurier | Ottawa/Hull | www.historymuseum.ca*

INSIDER TIP **DISCOVERY HARBOUR**
(146 C4) (⌂ *E13*)
The museum harbour on the shore of Lake Huron offers a great programme of activities: building model ships, learning to tie knots and mastering old sailing ships. *End June–Sept 10am–5pm | admission C$7, children C$5.25 | 93 Jury Dr. | Penetanguishene/Midland | www.discoveryharbour.on.ca*

DOON HERITAGE CROSSROADS
(146 B5) (⌂ *E13*)
Canadian country life on a hundred-year old farm: oxen pull the plough, geese cackle, and the (costumed) inhabitants live out the farmers' life in the restored houses. *In summer daily 9.30am–5pm |*

admission C$11, children C$5 | Hwy. 401, Exit 275 | Kitchener

MARINELAND (146 C5) (⌂ *E13*)
Large oceanarium with various whale and dolphin shows, aquariums, petting zoo and roller coasters. *End June–Aug daily 9am–6pm, beginning May–mid Oct 10am–5pm | admission C$48, children C$41 | 7657 Portage Rd. | Niagara Falls | marinelandcanada.com*

WHIRLPOOL JETBOAT TOURS ●
(146 C5) (⌂ *E13*)
Sparkling adventure for teenagers and parents: a wet and wild one-hour boat trip through the grade five rapids of the Niagara River. Bring a change of clothes along. *Admission C$61, children C$51 | 3850 Niagara Parkway | Niagara Falls | tel. 905 4 68 48 00 | www.whirlpooljet.com*

MONTRÉAL

PEPSI FORUM (U A5) (⌂ *a5*)
Perfect for teenagers: the old hockey stadium has been converted into a cinema complex that also includes a climbing wall, bowling alley, restaurants, a disco and trendy shops. *2313, Ste-Catherine Ouest | www.forum-montreal.com*

LA RONDE (147 F3) (⌂ *H12*)
A large amusement park on an island in the river. Several rollercoasters, bungee jumping and marionette shows as well as music stages. Also nice for smaller children. *Mid June–Aug daily 9.30am–10.30pm | admission C$67, children C$59 | Île Sainte-Hélène | www.laronde.com*

QUÉBEC

BENJO (148 B4) (⌂ *J11*)
The ultimate multi-storey shop for children: dolls, model aeroplanes, comput-

ers, young jugglers form the Cirque du Soleil, pottery courses and its own children's restaurant. *Mon–Fri from 10am, Sat/Sun from 9.30am | 550, Blvd. Charest Est. | Québec City | tel. 418 6 40 00 01 | www.benjo.ca*

PARC SAFARI (147 F3) (*⩕ H12*)

Large safari park with bears, wolves and African animal enclosures, also a water park, picnic sites and petting zoo. *Late June–early Sept daily 10am–7pm | admission C$39, children C$26 | Route 202 | Hemmingford | www.parcsafari.com*

ZOO SAUVAGE DE ST-FÉLICIEN (148 A2) (*⩕ J10*)

A true-to-nature animal park with many Canadian animals in large outdoor enclosures. *In summer daily 9am–7pm | admission C$39, children C$27 | 2230, Blvd. du Jardin | St-Félicien | www.zoosauvage.org*

ATLANTIC COAST

CAVENDISH (149 F4) (*⩕ N11*)

Resort in the north of P.E.I with a go-cart circuit, mini-golf (also in the dark: *Black Magic Minigolf*), a petting zoo and waterslides.

DISCOVERY CENTRE (149 F6) (*⩕ N13*)

A hands-on science centre with lots of experiments to try out. *Daily 10am–5pm, Wed until 8pm | admission C$12, children C$10 | 1593 Barrington St. | Halifax | www.discoverycentre.ns.ca*

SHUBENACADIE RIVER ADVENTURE TOURS (149 F5) (*⩕ N12*)

Exciting white water rafting trips on the wild rapids of the Shubenacadie in the Bay of Fundy – also mud slides! *10061 Hwy. 215 | South Maitland | tel. 902 2 61 22 22 | www.shubie.com*

Hot rollercoaster rides for adults, puppet shows for kids: La Ronde

FESTIVALS & EVENTS

In the summer and autumn festivals take place all over Eastern Canada – it is best to visit the local visitor's centre to find out what is being celebrated when and where. The public holidays are traditionally held on a Monday to make a long weekend. Victoria Day in late May and Labor Day in early September are two good reasons to take a short holiday.

FESTIVALS & EVENTS

FEBRUARY

Québec City: ⭐ *Carnaval du Québec.* Parades and regattas. *www.carnaval.qc.ca*

Ottawa: INSIDERTIP ▶ *Winterlude*. Ice-skating, ice sculptures and sled races

MAY

Ottawa: ⭐ *Canadian Tulip Festival.* Concerts, parade and of course beautiful blossoms

JUNE

Montréal: *Grand Prix du Canada.* On the 2nd weekend Formula 1 races in the home of Jacques Villeneuve; ⭐ *Festival International de Jazz* draws more than a thousand artists from all over the world. *www.montrealjazzfest.com*

Toronto: *Pride Week.* Three colourful costume parades on the last weekend are the highlight of the large gay festival. *www.pridetoronto.com*

JULY

Canada Day on July 1: Canada celebrates with picnics, parades and street festivals

Antigonish: *Highland Games* – in Nova Scotia with bagpipe music and caber tossing (2nd week)

Shediac: for five days in the middle of the month everything centres around the shellfish during the INSIDERTIP ▶ *Lobster Festival*. www.shediaclobsterfestival.ca

Montréal: during the comedy festival *Juste pour Rire*, comics and mimes perform over 14 days. *www.hahaha.com*

Québec City: *Festival d'Été.* Two weeks of theatre and concerts, a large French speaking cultural event. *www.infofestival.com*

Toronto: The *Caribana* is all about the Caribbean – for three weeks in mid July

AUGUST

Manitoulin Island: ⭐ **Wikwemikong Cultural Festival** with fascinating Ojibwa pow-wow dances and guest groups

Jazz & lobster festivals: ethnic groups and villages celebrate alongside the major festivals

from other tribes. *www.wikwemikong heritage.org*

Caraquet: The Atlantic province French-Canadians celebrate their history with the *Festival Acadien* in the first half of the month *festivalacadien.ca*

Toronto: *Canadian National Exhibition.* Canada largest fair takes place during the second half of the month

SEPTEMBER

Toronto: The annual mid-month *International Film Festival* shows approx. 300 films from 50 countries *tiff.net*

St Catharines: *Niagara Grape and Wine Festival.* Mid-month harvest festival with parade. *www.niagarawine festival.com*

OCTOBER

Kitchener: ⭐ *Oktoberfest.* German immigrants celebrate the largest beer festival in North America (2nd week). *www.oktoberfest.ca*

PUBLIC HOLIDAYS

1 Jan	New Year's Day, *Jour de l'An*
March/April Mon before	Good Friday, Easter
25 May	Victoria Day, *Jour de la Reine*
24 June	*Fête de la St-Jean-Baptiste* (National Holiday in Québec)
1 July	Canada Day, *Fête du Canada*
1st Mon in Aug	National Holiday (except Québec and Newfoundland)
1st Mon in Sept	Labour Day, *Fête du Travail*
2nd Mon in Oct	Thanksgiving, *Action de Grâce*
11 Nov	Remembrance Day, *Jour du Souvenir*
25/26 Dec	Christmas, *Noël*

LINKS, BLOGS, APPS & MORE

www.Canada.travel comprehensive site that includes videos, facebook and numerous links for travel details about places and regions to visit. Also recommendations by specially trained travel agents with experience of Canada

www.weather.gc.ca satellite imagery, rain radar – and amazingly precise weather forecasts for even the smallest town in this massive country

www.parkscanada.ca A good website with detailed descriptions of the individual national parks. The site includes videos, 3D representations and features such as an interactive map where you select your region for specials and highlights

www.thestar.com Toronto's online city magazine has good tips for restaurants, the hip and happening districts, events and music clubs

www.thecoast.ca Website of Halifax's trendy independent newspaper includes a concert calendar, links to videos, blogs about music, festivals, sports and alternative culture on the Atlantic

www.blogto.com Listings for current festivals, where to find the best food trucks, restaurant reviews, news from the art and music scene and much more from an independent group of Toronto locals. Montréal also has a similar site at www.midnightpoutine.ca

corridorcanada.ca This extensive web site offers information on all aspects of French Canada including culture, attractions and events

www.niagarablog.com News blog with a collection of articles, pictures, and videos about the Niagara Falls, also links to other blogs

ibackpackcanada.com A very informative and entertaining independent travel guide written by Corbin Fraser who decided to backpack from coast to coast for six months three years ago and hasn't stopped since. The ideal travel blog for all those interested in travelling through Canada on a budget.

Regardless of whether you are still researching your trip or already in Eastern Canada: these addresses will provide you with more information, videos and networks to make your holiday even more enjoyable

@EaterMontreal Tweets, photos and videos covering the restaurant and bar scene in Montréal. Often good advice for trendy cocktail clubs, ice cream shops and other meeting points

www.Flickr.com/photos/tags/Canada the photo bank (invented in Canada) offers numerous groups covering all tourist regions and topics. And you can also send pictures to your friends

www.airbnb.com An online booking site for guesthouses and private accommodation with lots of listings for Eastern Canada

www.vrbo.com and toronto.craigslist.ca cover privately rented accommodation in Toronto and other major towns of Canada. Also houses, apartments, etc. for several days

live.seetorontonow.com Like Toronto, numerous tourist offices of individual cities and provinces have now developd their own social media presence in Facebook, Instagram, Pinterest etc. Most offer information on attractions and current special offers

VIDEOS & MUSIC

www.cbc.ca/news/canada/newfoundland-labrador features the Newfoundland and Labrador section of the Canadian Radio Broadcasting site. Includes a lot of video articles on a variety of subjects. This includes short films, slide shows, photographs and news articles all showing life in Canada

www.Much.com Music videos and interviews with Canadian pop and rock stars from the most important music station in the country

www.cbcmusic.ca/#/radio3 All about Canada's music scene, indie bands and mainstream, up-to-date and with tips about upcoming concerts

APPS

Live Nation Information centre and tickets office for concert tours by leading stars and clubs and concert stages in Montreal and Toronto. Also iPhone app and Facebook service, details at www.livenation.com

OpenTable A useful app for restaurant reservations, with a good selection (especially in the cities) of restaurants; you can also use it to find restaurants closest to your current location and see what tables are available, last minute reservations are often an option

TRAVEL TIPS

ARRIVAL

✈ *Air Canada* and most national carriers have regular flights to Toronto and Montréal. The best option for flying to Newfoundland is with *Air Canada* via London. The same applies to Halifax. There are good flight connections to all the major cities in Eastern Canada and there are also numerous independent regional and local airlines that focus on the more remote regions.

The major car rental companies like *Avis*, *Hertz* and *Alamo/National* have representatives at all the airports. Taxis and airport buses are also available to take you into the city centre. If you have booked a mobile home, the rental company will usually collect you at the airport. An even better option is for you to first go into the city and then collect the vehicle the next morning – well-rested for your first trip with the unfamiliar vehicle.

RESPONSIBLE TRAVEL

It doesn't take a lot to be environmentally friendly whilst travelling. Don't just think about your carbon footprint whilst flying to and from your holiday destination, but also about how you can protect nature and culture abroad. As a tourist it is especially important to respect nature, look out for local products, cycle instead of driving, save water and much more. If you would like to find out more about eco-tourism please visit: *www.ecotourism.org*

B&BS, HOLIDAY HOMES

Log cabins on the coast or in the woods, B & Bs in Victorian villas, city apartments and cosy country estates as house swaps: the choice of accommodation beyond regular hotels is varied. B & Bs are often available on short notice and easy to book via Airbnb or at the local information centres. They can also be found on websites such as: *www.bbcanada.com* or *www.canadianbandbguide.ca.*

Holiday houses or apartments are popular for stays of a week or longer, and are especially popular in the Muskoka Lake region north of Toronto and on the coast in the Atlantic provinces. They can also be found on websites like: *www.cottages incanada.com* or *www.vrbo.com.* And if you are ready to offer your own home and swap it with the Canadians, you can look on the following websites: *www. homeexchange.com* or *www.homelink. org/canada*

BUS & TRAIN

Greyhound and regional bus lines such as *Megabus* connect all major towns. Another way to see Canada is to travel from coast to coast by train. The route from Toronto to Vancouver must be booked a few months in advance! Further lines travel from Montréal to the Gaspésie Peninsula and Halifax. The railroad company *VIA Rail* offers a *Canrailpass* for their entire network and a *Corridorpass* for Québec and Ontario. In 2010 all long-distance trains were refurbished.

There are a number of privately operated regional train services such as the

From arrival to weather

Your holiday from start to finish: the most important addresses and information for your trip to Eastern Canada

Ontario Northland (www.ontarionorth land.ca) offering the seasonal *Polar Bear Express*.

Trains may be a pricey option but rail services often have special deals. A round-trip ticket is cheaper than a one-way fare and there are further significant savings if you buy tickets well in advance. See the *VIA Rail* website *(www. viarail.ca)* for further promotions and vacation packages.

CAMPING & YOUTH HOSTELS

Canada's public camping sites are beautiful, they are usually situated next to the water in national parks and they all have a fireplace, wooden benches, water pump and a simple outhouse and cost C$10–30 per night. Private, luxuriously equipped sites can be found on the outskirts of cities and outside of national parks (prices approx. C$15–45). Wild camping is not prohibited (except in the parks), but is frowned upon in the populated areas.

Accommodations from the *Canadian Hostelling Association (www.hihostels. ca)* cost from C$21 per night, some offer single and double rooms from C$46. Backpackers can stay at the *YMCA* (men) and the *YWCA* (women) in cities, in the countryside you often find small hostels.

CAR HIRE

Minimum age for a rental is 21, often 25 years. Your national licence will suffice. Cars or campers should be booked a few months in advance. It is often cheaper and safer, as mobile homes are often fully booked in the summer.

CONSULATES & EMBASSIES

BRITISH HIGH COMMISSION
80 Elgin Street | Ottawa | ON K1P 5K7| tel. +1 613 2 377 15 30 | ukincanada.fco.gov.uk

U.S. EMBASSY
490 Sussex Drive | Ottawa | ON K1N 1G8 | tel. +1 613 6 88 53 35 | ca.usembassy.gov

AUSTRALIAN HIGH COMMISSION
Suite 1301 | 50 O'Connor Street | Ottawa | ON K1P 6L2 | tel. +1 613 2 36 08 41 | www. canada.embassy.gov.au

CONSUMING ALCOHOL

Buying and consuming alcohol in Canada is not as straightforward as in other parts of the world. You can buy beer and wine at some licensed grocery stores in certain provinces, but stronger alcoholic beverages have to be purchased in government stores *(Société des Alcools)*. Many restaurants have a liquor license and those without a license usually allow customers to bring their own wine – look for the 'Apportez votre vin/Bring Your Own' signs. Each province and territory has their own drinking age (usually 18 or 19). It is also generally prohibited to consume alcohol in public places, and in some provinces it is even forbidden to carry open non-empty alcohol containers within a parked car.

CUSTOMS

The following goods can be imported duty free into Canada: 1.1 litres of spirits, 200 cigarettes and gifts up to a value of C$60. Plants and foodstuffs, especially fresh food, may not be imported.

DOMESTIC FLIGHTS & FERRY ROUTES

Air Canada and some regional airlines frequently offer discounted rates for intra-Canadian routes via internet sales. It is also advantageous to include domestic routes in transatlantic tickets.

The ferries that operate on the St Lawrence in Québec and to P.E.I. operate hourly and you need not book in advance. However, it is necessary to make a reservation in advance for the car ferries to Sydney/Nova Scotia and to Newfoundland and in the summer from Tobermory to Manitoulin Island in Lake Huron (bookings at travel agencies and all Canadian tour operators; info at *www.marine-atlantic.ca* and *www.ontarioferries.com)*.

BUDGETING

Coffee	£1.80–3.10/US$2.50–4.30	*for a pot of coffee*
Beer	£3.50–5.30/US$4.90–7.40	*for a beer in a restaurant*
Lobster	£18–31/US$24.50–43	*for a lobster with side dish*
Jeans	£35–62/US$49–86	*for Levi's or Wrangler*
Tour	£45–70/US$60–100	*for a half-day raft or bicycle trip*
Petrol	£0.75–0.80/US$1.05–1.10	*1 litre unleaded*

DRIVING

You can drive with your national driver's licence for up to three months. In all provinces it is compulsory to wear seatbelts. The road network is in a good condition, but the north of the provinces has fewer roads. The maximum speed on major roads is 80 km/49.7 mi or 100 km/62 mi, in towns 50 km/31.1 mi and on motorways 110 km/68 mi. Traffic regulations are standard with certain unusual features: at the traffic light you can also turn right on red (not in Montréal), on multi-lane roads you may overtake but schoolbuses with their hazards lights on may never be passed, not even from the opposite side. The legal blood alcohol limit is 0.8.

The *Canadian Automobile Association (CAA)* also helps members of foreign clubs (with maps and tips, but not in case of a break-down).

ELECTRICITY

Current is 110 volts, 60Hz. Appliances such as mobile/tablet, shavers and hair dryers from other countries will need a transformer and you will also need a plug adaptor for Canada's two-pin sockets.

EMERGENCY SERVICES

911 or dial *0* for the operator

HEALTH

Medical care in Canada is very good – but expensive. A day in the hospital can cost C$1000 or more. Ensure that you have foreign health insurance. Medicine can be bought in a pharmacy or drugstore.

IMMIGRATION

Tourists from the USA, EU countries and most Commonwealth countries (UK, Australia and New Zealand) only need a valid passport to enter Canada (machine readable and with biometric data) and since 2016 also the *Electronic Travel Authorization (ETA)* – available for C$7 *at www.canada.ca/eta*.) – passport holders from other countries must apply for visas.

The immigration officer at your point of arrival decides your length of stay – generally not longer than six months.

If you decide to extend your stay once you have arrived in Canada, you will need to apply for an extension at the nearest Canada Immigration Centre. You will need to do this well in advance of the expiry of your current authorised date. If you plan to cross the border into the US, first check to see if you qualify to enter under the Visa Waiver Program (VWP), which allows you to travel to the US for 90 days or fewer without having to obtain a visa.

INFORMATION

The Canadian Tourist Office website *www. canada.travel* provides extensive information about Canada's attractions and activities. There are also competitions and travel ideas. There are links to the individual provinces, such as Ontario and Nova Scotia and you can also request brochures and maps for each region.

In Canada itself you will find well signposted *Info Centres* and *Visitors Bureaus* that will provide you with maps and tips.

TOURISM NEW BRUNSWICK

P.O. Box 6000, Fredericton, NB E3B 5H1 | tel. +1 800 5610123 | www.tourismnew brunswick.ca

NEWFOUNDLAND AND LABRADOR TOURISM

P.O. Box 8700, St John's, NL A1B 4J6 | tel. +1 709 729 28 30 (*, outside NA), +1 800 563 63 53 (inside NA) | www.newfound landlabrador.com

TOURISM NOVA SCOTIA

P.O. Box 667, Windsor, BON 2T0 | tel. 902 742 05 11 (*, outside NA and local), +1 800 565 00 00 (insde NA) | www.novascotia.com

CURRENCY CONVERTER

£	C$	C$	£
1	1.75	1	0.55
3	5.25	3	1.65
5	8.75	5	2.75
20	35	20	11
40	70	40	22
75	131.25	75	41.25
200	350	200	110
500	875	500	275

C$	US$	US$	C$
1	0.75	1	1.30
3	2.25	3	3.90
5	3.75	5	6.50
20	15	20	26
40	30	40	52
75	56.25	75	97.50
200	150	200	260
500	375	500	650

For current exchange rates see www.xe.com

P.E.I. DEPARTMENT OF TOURISM

P.O. Box 2000, Charlottetown, PE C1A 7N8 | tel. +1 902 437 85 70 (outside NA), +1 800 463 47 34 (inside NA) | www. princeedwardisland.ca

INTERNET & WI-FI

Canada has a well-established network. High-speed internet access can cost between C$10 and 15 a day. Many motels and smaller hotels have a computer in the lobby available for guests who can view emails and print route maps free of charge.

With your own laptop, smart phone or tablet you will find Wi-Fi in various hotels, cafés, vistor centres and public places. Most of the time the network is free of charge and freely available, but sometimes you have to pay a fee to get the password from staff.

MONEY & CREDIT CARDS

Local currency is the Canadian dollar (= 100 cents). Bank notes are available in 5, 10, 20, 50 and 100 dollars and coins in ¢1 (penny), ¢5 (nickel), ¢10 (dime), ¢25 (quarter), C$1 and C$2. Banks are usually open from 10am to 3pm. They cash traveller's cheques (made out in Canadian or US dollars), but do not exchange any other currency. You can exchange foreign currencies into dollars at airports and major hotels (but the rate may be bad). Divide your holiday fund into various payment methods: approx. C$100 cash for the arrival, a credit card for the majority of daily expenses (Visa or Mastercard is accepted everywhere at petrol stations, restaurants, etc.), as well as a debit cards which you can use to draw cash from most ATMs at a favourable exchange rate. To be on the safe side, you can also take a few hundred dollars in traveller's cheques (they are accepted in shops and restaurants and you get your change in cash).

OPENING HOURS

Shops are generally open Mon–Sat from 9.30am–6pm, large malls Mon–Sat 10am–9pm, Sun noon–5pm and supermarkets are often also open evenings and weekends, while in larger cities some are open 24 hours. Many museums are closed on Mondays.

POST

Post offices are open Mon–Fri 9am–6pm and Sat 8am–12pm. It costs ¢61 for letters and postcards within Canada, C$1.05 to the US and C$2.50 for international mail (up to 30g).

WEATHER IN MONTRÉAL

	Jan	Feb	March	April	May	June	July	Aug	Sept	Oct	Nov	Dec
Daytime temperatures in °C/F°	−5/23	−5/23	2/26	10/50	18/64	23/73	26/79	25/77	19/66	13/55	5/41	−3/27
Nighttime temperatures in °C/F°	−13/9	−13/9	−6/21	5/41	8/46	14/75	17/63	16/61	11/52	5/41	−1/30	−10/1
☀	3	4	5	6	7	7	8	7	6	4	2	2
☂	10	11	7	8	10	9	10	10	7	10	12	12

PHONE & MOBILE PHONE

European tri- or quad-band phones also function in Canada – but usually only in the cities and in the south of the provinces. Contact your mobile phone provider bevore travelling to find out about special rates. Beware: always turn off the internet access roaming feature on your smart phone otherwise you can run up some high charges.

You can make inexpensive phone calls from your hotel with a prepaid long distance phone card which can be purchased locally at kiosks and small supermarkets. For longer stays it is worth getting a local SIM card for your (unlocked!) mobile phone from the Canadian GSM providers such as *Fido* or *Rogers*.

All the telephone numbers in Canada have seven digits, when dialling any number (local or long distance) you must include the area code.

Local calls from telephone booths cost C$0.25–0.35. For long distance a computerised voice will tell you the charge after you have chosen an option. Beware: hotels often have horrendous surcharges! The operator (dial *0*) will help you with any telephone problems and also sets up collect calls.

Toll free numbers to book hotels or tours start with the prefix *800*, *866*, *877* or *888*.

TAX

Canada has a 5 per cent *Goods and Services Tax (GST)* but there are also additional regional taxes, some of which are only added to the purchase price at the cashier, such as in Québec. In Ontario and the Atlantic provinces all the taxes are combined into one *Harmonized Sales Tax (HST)* of 12–15 per cent.

TIME ZONE

Canada has multiple time zones. Newfoundland is on *Newfoundland Time* (3.5 hours behind UK and 1.5 hours ahead of Eastern US). The Maritimes and Labrador are on *Atlantic Standard Time* (4 hours behind UK and 1 hour ahead of Eastern US). Québec and most of Ontario are on *Eastern Standard Time* (5 hours behind UK), which is the same time zone as New York and Eastern US. Daylight Saving Time begins at 2am local time on the second Sunday in March. On the first Sunday in November Daylight Saving Time returns to Standard Time at 2am local time.

TIPPING

The tip is not included in the restaurant and the standard amount is 15–18 per cent. Hotel porters get about C$1–2 per piece of baggage.

WEIGHTS & MEASURES

Canada uses the metric system, distances are in kilometres, temperatures in Celsius and products are sold in grams, kilograms or litres.

WHEN TO GO

Apart from the Atlantic coast and the St Lawrence Valley Eastern Canada has an extreme climate which ensures cold winters and hot summers. The best time to travel (and high season) is mid-June to late August. May and September, however, are just as nice – with sunny days and cool nights. And in autumn the vibrant colours of the forest foliage are beautiful. February and March are best for snowmobiling and cross-country skiing.

USEFUL PHRASES FRENCH

IN BRIEF

Yes/No/Maybe	oui/non/peut-être
Please/Thank you	s'il vous plaît/merci
Good morning!/afternoon!/ evening!/night!	Bonjour!/Bonjour!/ Bonsoir!/Bonne nuit!
Hello!/goodbye!/See you!	Salut!/Au revoir!/Salut!
Excuse me, please	Pardon!
My name is ...	Je m'appelle ...
I'm from ...	Je suis de ...
May I ...?/Pardon?	Puis-je ...?/Comment?
I would like to .../have you got ...?	Je voudrais .../Avez-vous?
How much is ...?	Combien coûte ...?
I (don't) like this	Ça (ne) me plaît (pas).
good/bad/broken	bon/mauvais/cassé
too much/much/little	trop/beaucoup/peu
all/nothing	tout/rien
Help!/Attention!	Au secours/attention
police/fire brigade/ ambulance	police/pompiers/ ambulance
Could you please help me?	Est-ce que vous pourriez m'aider?
Do you speak English?	Parlez-vous anglais?
Do you understand?	Est-ce que vous comprenez?
Could you please ...?	Pourriez vous ... s'il vous plait?
... repeat that	répéter
... speak more slowly	parler plus lentement
... write that down	l'écrire

DATE & TIME

Monday/Tuesday	lundi/mardi
Wednesday/Thursday	mercredi/jeudi
Friday/Saturday/Sunday	vendredi/samedi/dimanche
working day/holiday	jour ouvrable/jour férié
today/tomorrow/yesterday	aujourd'hui/demain/hier
hour/minute	heure/minute
day/night/week	jour/nuit/semaine
month/year	mois/année
What time is it?	Quelle heure est-t-il?
It's three o'clock	Il est trois heures
It's half past three.	Il est trois heures et demi
a quarter to four	quatre heures moins le quart

Parlez-vous français?

'Do you speak French?' This guide will help you to say the basic words and phrases in French.

TRAVEL

open/closed	ouvert/fermé
entrance/exit	entrée/sortie
departure/arrival	départ/arrivée
toilets/restrooms/ ladies/gentlemen	toilettes/ femmes/hommes
(no) drinking water	eau (non) potable
Where is ...?/ Where are ...?	Où est ...?/ Où sont ...?
left/right	à gauche/à droite
straight ahead/back	tout droit/en arrière
close/far	près/loin
bus/tram/underground/ taxi/cab	bus/tramway/ métro/taxi
stop/cab stand	arrêt/station de taxi
parking lot/parking garage	parking
street map/map	plan de ville/carte routière
train station/harbour/ airport	gare/port/ aéroport
schedule/ticket	horaire/billet
single/return	aller simple/aller-retour
train/track/platform	train/voie/quai
I would like to rent ... a car/a bicycle/ a boat	Je voudrais ... louer une voiture/un vélo/ un bateau

FOOD & DRINK

The menu, please	La carte, s'il vous plaît
Could I please have ...?	Puis-je avoir ... s'il vous plaît
bottle/carafe/glass	bouteille/carafe/verre
knife/fork/spoon	couteau/fourchette/cuillère
salt/pepper/sugar	sel/poivre/sucre
vinegar/oil	vinaigre/huile
milk/cream/lemon	lait/crème/citron
cold/too salty/not cooked	froid/trop salé/pas cuit

with/without ice/sparkling	avec/sans glaçons/gaz
vegetarian	végétarien(ne)
May I have the bill, please	Je voudrais payer, s'il vous plaît
bill	addition

SHOPPING

pharmacy/chemist	pharmacie/droguerie
baker/market	boulangerie/marché
shopping centre	centre commercial
department store	grand magasin
100 grammes/1 kilo	cent grammes/un kilo
expensive/cheap/price	cher/bon marché/prix
more/less	plus/moins
organically grown	de l'agriculture biologique

ACCOMMODATION

I have booked a room	J'ai réservé une chambre
Do you have any ... left?	Avez-vous encore ...?
single room/double room	chambre simple/double
breakfast	petit déjeuner
half board/full board (American plan)	demi-pension/pension complète
shower/sit-down bath	douche/bain
balcony/terrace	balcon/terrasse
key/room card	clé/carte magnétique
luggage/suitcase/bag	bagages/valise/sac

BANKS, MONEY & CREDIT CARDS

bank/ATM/pin code	banque/guichet automatique/code
cash/credit card	comptant/carte de crédit
bill/coin	billet/monnaie

HEALTH

doctor/dentist/	médecin/dentiste/
paediatrician	pédiatre
hospital/emergency clinic	hôpital/urgences
fever/pain	fièvre/douleurs
diarrhoea/nausea	diarrhée/nausée
sunburn	coup de soleil
inflamed/injured	enflammé/blessé
plaster/bandage	pansement/bandage
ointment/pain reliever	pommade/analgésique

POST, TELECOMMUNICATIONS & MEDIA

stamp	timbre
letter/postcard	lettre/carte postale
I need a landline phone card	J'ai besoin d'une carte téléphonique pour fixe.
I'm looking for a prepaid card for my mobile	Je cherche une recharge pour mon portable.
Where can I find internet access?	Où puis-je trouver un accès à internet?
dial/connection/engaged	composer/connection/occupé
socket/charger	prise électrique/chargeur
computer/battery/ rechargeable battery	ordinateur/batterie/ accumulateur
at sign (@)	arobase
internet address (URL)/ e-mail address	adresse internet/ mail
internet connection/wi-fi	accès internet/wi-fi
e-mail/file/print	mail/fichier/imprimer

LEISURE, SPORTS & BEACH

beach	plage
sunshade/lounger	parasol/transat
low tide/high tide/current	marée basse/marée haute/courant
cable car/chair lift	téléphérique/télésiège
(rescue) hut	refuge

NUMBERS

0	zéro	17	dix-sept
1	un, une	18	dix-huit
2	deux	19	dix-neuf
3	trois	20	vingt
4	quatre	30	trente
5	cinq	40	quarante
6	six	50	cinquante
7	sept	60	soixante
8	huit	70	soixante-dix
9	neuf	80	quatre-vingt
10	dix	90	quatre-vingt-dix
11	onze	100	cent
12	douze	200	deux cents
13	treize	1000	mille
14	quatorze		
15	quinze	½	un[e] demi[e]
16	seize	¼	un quart

ROAD ATLAS

The green line indicates the Discovery Tour 'Eastern Canada at a glance'
The blue line indicates the other Discovery Tours

All tours are also marked on the pull-out map

142 Photo: Thousand Islands

Exploring Eastern Canada

The map on the back cover shows how the area has been sub-divided

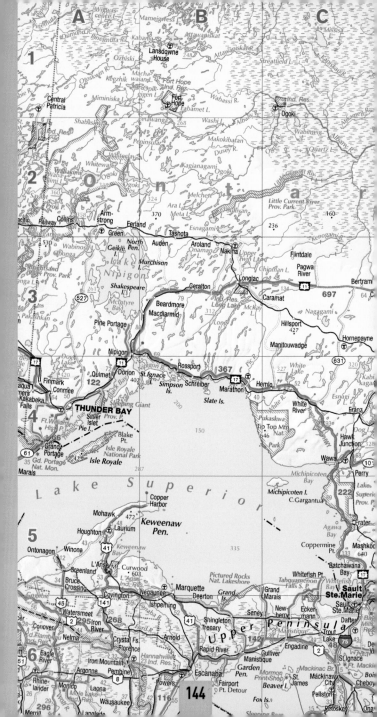

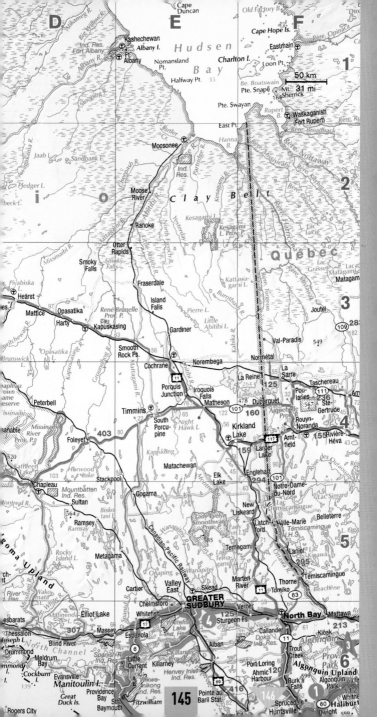

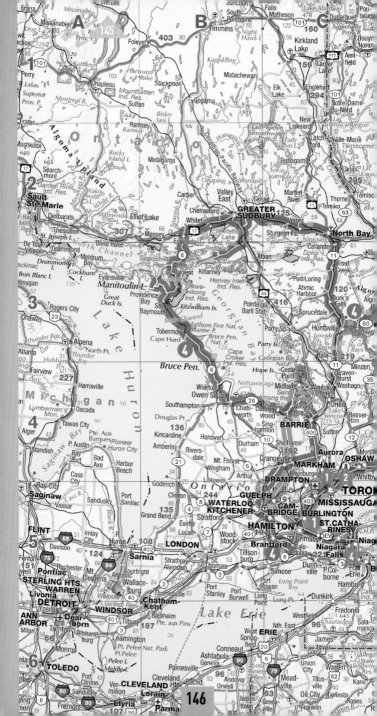

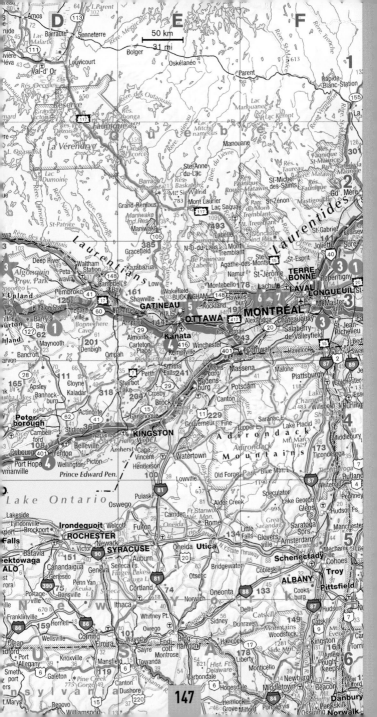

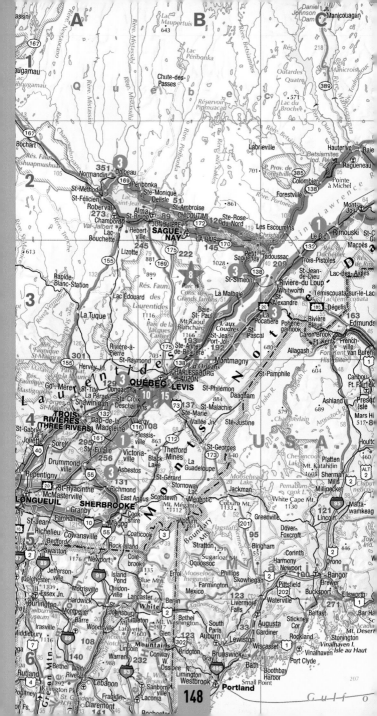

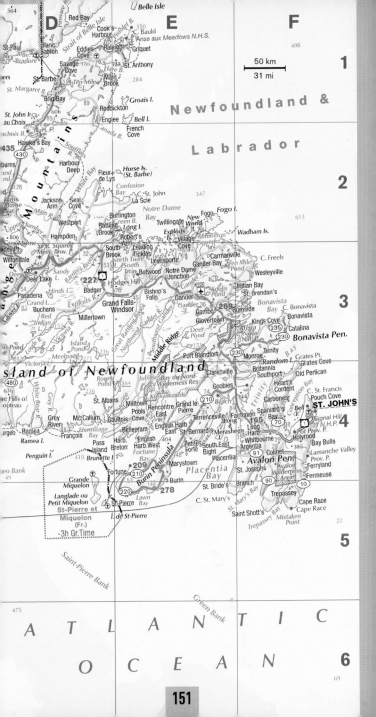

D

Belle Isle
Red Bay
Cook's-Harbour
C. Bauld
St-Paul
Blanc-Sablon
Anse aux Meadows N.H.S.
Eddies Cove
Raleigh
Griquet
St. Anthony
Savage Cove
186
Main Brook
St. Barbe
Ten Mile
284

E

F

498

1

50 km
31 mi

Newfoundland &

L a b r a d o r

St. Margaret B.
St. John I.
au Choix
606
Brig Bay
89
Roddickton
Groais I.
Hawke's Bay
430
435
126
Harbour Deep
Fleur-de-Lys
Horse Is. (St. Barbe)
347
613
Soufflets B.
Jackson Arm
Cove
Confusion Bay
St. John
Westport
Main R.
Burlington
La Scie
Notre Dame
Fogo I.
Fogo
Wadham Is.
Hampden
Green B.
Long I.
Twillingate
New World I.
Robert's Arm
Exploits
Is.
Village Cove
C. Freels
South Brook
Leading Tickles
Carmanville
Wesleyville
Lewisporte
Gander Bay
Ten Mile
227
Hodges Hill
Botwood
Notre Dame Junction
Indian Bay
St-Brendan's
Bishop's Falls
Gander
36
269
Burnside
Bonavista Bay
C. Bonavista
Badger
370
Grand Falls-Windsor
Gambo
Glovertown
Kings Cove
235
Bonavista
Millertown
Buchans
Red
Indian
Deer Pond
Terra Nova Nat. P.
Catalina
Bonavista Pen.

3

Island of Newfoundland
Middle Ridge
Port Blandford
230
Trinity
Monroe
Random I.
Grates Pt.
Grates Cove
Old Perlican
480
Round Pond
364
Jubilee
Bay du Nord Wilderness Res.
Clarenville
Britannia
Southport
Heart's Content
Carbonear
C. St. Francis
Pouch Cove
N.H.P.
St. Albans
Milltown
74
210
Goobies
144
Fairhaven
Spaniard's Bay
70
Bell
ST. JOHN'S
Signal Hill N.H.P.
McCallum
Pools Cove
Grand le Pierre
Rencontre East
Terrenceville
Long Harb.
Holyrood
Bay Bulls
Belleoram
English Harb.
English Harb. West
404
St. Bernard's
Petite Forte
South East Bight
Masareen
Whitbourne
Argentia
91
Colinet
Lamanche Valley Prov. P.
Ferryland
209
Fortune
210
Brunette I.
Marystown
Placentia Bay
Placentia
St. Josephs
Avalon Pen.
Avalon Wilderness Area
90
10
Fermeuse
Grande Miquelon
Langlade ou Petit Miquelon
278
220
Burin
St. Bride's
Branch
C. St. Mary's
Trepassey
Cape Race
St-Pierre et Miquelon (Fr.)
-3h Gr.Time
St-Pierre
I. de St-Pierre
Lawn Bay
Saint Shott's
St. Mary's Bay
Trepassey Bay
Mistaken Point
22

5

Saint-Pierre Bank

A T L A N T I C

Green Bank

O C E A N

69

6

151

KEY TO ROAD ATLAS

German / English		French / Spanish
Autobahn, mehrspurige Straße - in Bau Highway, multilane divided road - under construction		Autoroute, route à plusieurs voies - en construction Autopista, carretera de más carriles - en construcción
Fernverkehrsstraße - in Bau Trunk road - under construction		Route à grande circulation - en construction Ruta de larga distancia - en construcción
Hauptstraße Principal highway		Route principale Carretera principal
Nebenstraße Secondary road		Route secondaire Carretera secundaria
Fahrweg, Piste Practicable road, track		Chemin carrossable, piste Camino vecinal, pista
Straßennummerierung Road numbering	① **48** ☊ ㉖ **㉖**	Numérotage des routes Numeración de carreteras
Entfernungen in mi. (USA), in km (CDN) Distances in mi. (USA), in km (CDN)	**259** 130 ⁄ 129	Distances en mi. (USA), en km (CDN) Distancias en mi. (USA), en km (CDN)
Höhe in Meter - Pass Height in meters - Pass	1365 •	Altitude en mètres - Col Altura en metros - Puerto de montaña
Eisenbahn Railway		Chemin-de-fer Ferrocarril
Autofähre - Schifffahrtslinie Car ferry - Shipping route		Bac autos - Ligne maritime Transportador de automóviles - Ferrocarriles
Wichtiger internationaler Flughafen - Flughafen Major international airport - Airport	✈ ✈	Aéroport important international - Aéroport Aeropuerto importante internacional - Aeropuerto
Internationale Grenze - Bundesstaatengrenze International boundary - federal boundary		Frontière nationale - Frontière fédérale Frontera nacional - Frontera federal
Unbestimmte Grenze Undefined boundary		Frontière d'État non définie Frontera indeterminada
Zeitzonengrenze Time zone boundary	-4h Greenwich Time -3h Greenwich Time	Limite de fuseau horaire Límite del huso horario
Hauptstadt eines souveränen Staates National capital	**OTTAWA**	Capitale nationale Capital de un estado soberano
Hauptstadt einer Provinz Provincial capital	**TORONTO**	Capitale d'un chef-lieu Capital de provincia
Sperrgebiet Restricted area		Zone interdite Zona prohibida
Indianerreservat - Nationalpark Indian reservation - National park		Réserve d'indiens - Parc national Reserva de indios - Parque nacional
Sehenswertes Kulturdenkmal Interesting cultural monument	✳ *Disneyland*	Monument culturel intéressant Monumento cultural de interés
Sehenswertes Naturdenkmal Interesting natural monument	✳ *Niagara Falls*	Monument naturel intéressant Monumento natural de interés
Brunnen, Salzsee Well, Salt lake	◡	Puits, Lac salé Pozo, Lago salado
MARCO POLO Erlebnistour 1 MARCO POLO Discovery Tour 1		MARCO POLO Tour d'aventure 1 MARCO POLO Recorrido aventura 1
MARCO POLO Erlebnistouren MARCO POLO Discovery Tours		MARCO POLO Tours d'aventure MARCO POLO Recorridos de aventura
MARCO POLO Highlight	★1	MARCO POLO Highlight

MARCO POLO TRAVEL GUIDES

INDEX

This index lists all sights, destinations and lakes featured in this guide. Numbers in bold indicate a main entry.

CREDITS

WRITE TO US

e-mail: info@marcopologuides.co.uk
Did you have a great holiday? Is there something on your mind? Whatever it is, let us know! Whether you want to praise, alert us to errors or give us a personal tip – MARCO POLO would be pleased to hear from you. We do everything we can to provide the very latest information for your trip.

Nevertheless, despite all of our authors' thorough research, errors can creep in. MARCO POLO does not accept any liability for this. Please contact us by e-mail or post.

MARCO POLO Travel Publishing Ltd
Pinewood, Chineham Business Park
Crockford Lane, Chineham
Basingstoke, Hampshire RG24 8AL
United Kingdom

PICTURE CREDITS
Cover photograph: Lac Blanc (huber-images: A. Biscaro)
Photos: Alumnae Theatre Company: Joshua Meles (18 centre); Brasserie Benelux: Bianca Robitaille (18 top); DuMont Bildarchiv: Widmann (30/31, 62); huber-images: Biscaro (7), A. Biscaro (1 top, 19 top), P. Canali (5, 11, 12/13, 20/21, 32/33, 36, 38/39, 41, 44/45, 50, 54, 60, 68/69, 74, 130 top), M. Carassale (123), C. Irek (90), S. Kremer (58/59, 65, 70, 76, 81), R. Mirau (131), Schmid (26/27, 29, 79, 89, 94/95), R. Schmid (4, 14/15, 84/85 86, 103, 130 bottom); Laif: Grive (6), Heeb (front flap left), Le Figaro Magazine (Fautre) (1 top), Linkel (120/121), Raach (22, 30, 67); Laif/Arcticphoto (124/125); Laif/Aurora: McLain (17); Laif/hemis.fr (10, 28 left, 31, 114/115, 128, 128/129, 129); Laif/Polaris (34); mauritius images/age (92); mauritius images/Alamy (2/3, 28 right, 43, 46, 73, 97, 100, 104/105, 108, 111, 127, 146/147), P. Collis (19 bottom), R. Hicker (98/99), B. Yuanyue Bi (8); mauritius images/Alamy/Stockimo/iaarts (25); mauritius images/Imagebroker: O. Maksymenko (49), T. Sbampato (56, 119); mauritius images/SuperStock (82/83); Société de transport de Montréal: Michel E. Tremblay (18 bottom); K. Teuschl (9); T. P. Widmann (front flap right, 53)

3rd edition 2019
fully revised and updated
Worldwide Distribution: Marco Polo Travel Publishing Ltd, Pinewood, Chineham Business Park, Crockford Lane, Basingstoke, Hampshire RG24 8AL, United Kingdom. E-mail: sales@marcopolouk.com
© MAIRDUMONT GmbH & Co. KG, Ostfildern
Chief editor: Marion Zorn
Author: Karl Teuschl; editor: Marlis v. Hessert-Fraatz
Programme supervision: Lucas Forst-Gill, Susanne Heimburger, Tamara Hub, Johanna Jiranek, Nikolai Michaelis, Kristin Wittemann, Tim Wohlbold
Picture editor: Gabriele Forst
What's hot: Karl Teuschl and wunder media, Munich
Cartography road atlas & pull-out map: © MAIRDUMONT, Ostfildern
Cover design, p. 1, pull-out map cover: Karl Anders – Studio für Brand Profiling, Hamburg; design inside: milchhof:atelier, Berlin; p 2/3, Discovery Tours: Susan Chaaban Dipl.-Des. (FH)
Translated from German by Wendy Barrow, Lindsay Chalmers-Gerbracht and Rupert Kindermann
Editorial office: SAW Communications, Redaktionsbüro Dr. Sabine A. Werner, Mainz: Angela Atkinson, Julia Gilcher, Dr. Sabine A. Werner; prepress: SA W Communications, Mainz, in cooperation with alles mit Medien, Mainz Phrase book in cooperation with Ernst Klett Sprachen GmbH, Stuttgart, Editorial by Pons Wörterbücher

MIX
Paper from responsible sources
FSC® C124385

DOS & DON'TS ✋

A few things you should bear in mind on your holiday

DON'T SPEAK ENGLISH IN QUÉBEC

In Montréal and Québec City one hears English everywhere. But in Québec's hinterland, especially in the heartland of the separatists around Chicoutimi and Lac Saint-Jean, English is unpopular.

DON'T UNDERESTIMATE DISTANCES

Canada is a massive country and the distances on a map can be deceiving. Especially in the vast north of the country where a finger breadth on the map can mean a very long day trip on seemingly endless dirt roads.

DO INFORM AUTHORITIES BEFORE YOU GO ON A HIKE

Whether it is just for a day, a week or an entire month that you are going for a hike or canoe trip: always leave a note with your hiking or canoeing route and the time of your return. Leave the information with canoe rentals, the bush pilots that take you into the hinterland, or with the wardens in the national parks. All police stations (RCMP) will also accept these notes. If indeed something does go wrong, a search party can be sent out immediately. Please do not forget to report back once you have returned safely.

DO DRIVE SLOWLY NEAR SCHOOLS

The traffic signs are very clear: you are only allowed to drive 30 km/18 mph near schools. Stick to the limit as the

Mounties are very strict about this law. In July and August the schools are on holiday, but during all the other months you are only allowed to drive at a snail's pace close to schools. Keep a look out for school buses with hazard lights. You are not allowed to overtake them – not even from the opposite direction!

DO REMEMBER THE MOSQUITO REPELLENT

Do not go hiking without mosquito repellent in the Canadian bush – the mosquitoes will have a field day with you! A simple small bottle of *Off, Muskol* or *Cutter* will make all the difference and keep mosquitoes off.

WADE SAFELY THROUGH COASTAL MUDFLATS

It is said you should never turn your back to the Atlantic. This is sound advice. Freak waves can occur at any time on rocky coasts such as those in Newfoundland or around Peggy's Cove. Take especial care in the Bay of Fundy: with tidal differences of up to 15 m/ 49.2 ft, the tide can rush in at the speed of a bicycle – fatal for reckless waders on the coastal mudflats.

DON'T DRIVE UNDER THE INFLUENCE OF ALCOHOL

Although the blood alcohol limit is 0.8, the insurance company will not pay out in the event of an accident. In addition, the police will show no mercy and the penalties are draconian.